MORE THAN PETTICOATS

REMARKABLE MASSACHUSETTS WOMEN

Lura Rogers Seavey

TWODOT®

GUILFORD, CONNECTICUT
HELENA, MONTANA
AN IMPRINT OF THE GLOBE PEQUOT PRESS

For Cita, whose passion for history and thirst for knowledge has inspired many.

To buy books in quantity for corporate use
or incentives, call **(800) 962–0973, ext. 4551,**
or e-mail **premiums@GlobePequot.com.**

A · TWODOT® · BOOK

Copyright © 2005 by The Globe Pequot Press

Cover photo: A team of Canning Club girls training, 1916. Courtesy of the Massachusetts Historical Society.

Library of Congress Cataloging-in-Publication Data is available.

ISBN 0-7627-2599-0

Manufactured in the United States of America
First Edition/First Printing

CONTENTS

INTRODUCTION

*M*assachusetts has been home to some of America's richest historical events. The people of Massachusetts have a history of being trailblazers—courageous and innovative while benefiting from the state's important role in the nation's birth and its incredible concentration of great minds. In choosing the women for this book, it was difficult to decide between such incredible figures as the poet Emily Dickinson; the courageous Mary Rowlandson, who was kidnapped and later ransomed by Native Americans; and the founder of the American kindergarten system, Elizabeth Palmer Peabody. Many women from the state have made incredible contributions to our world and led interesting, unusual, and often interconnected lives. The women finally selected for inclusion in this volume were chosen not only for merit and accomplishment but as an opportunity to relate stories that are not often heard. Thus, lesser-known women were selected over those who have had fame. Many of these women triumphed over nearly impossible circumstances, all the while reminding us that they were mere humans. Others challenged women's traditional roles in society during times when this meant going against all they had been taught. Their stories include the families and friends who supported them with confidence; some women were encouraged by the men in their lives and others—like Abigail Adams—prove true the notion that behind every great man is a greater woman.

The effect that these women's lives have had on the course of society is undeniable. They paved the way for legal reform and helped shape the face of equality. The foundations they laid have

made it possible for others to follow in their footsteps and continue to challenge both themselves and others. They have given
confidence to subsequent generations and are role models for
every woman.

ELIZABETH "MUMBET" FREEMAN
1744?–1829

Pioneer of Emancipation

For 3 long miles the woman trudged through snow and ice from the Ashley house to Sheffield, the weather ironically comforting to her freshly burned skin. She was greeted with some surprise at the home of the young lawyer Theodore Sedgwick, who knew her only as his friend's slave and servant. With confidence and dignity, she exposed her wounded arm and proposed a lawsuit against her captors, John and Hannah Ashley. The suit, she said, should be based on the new Declaration of Rights in the Massachusetts Constitution. Theodore was astonished. He knew this woman to be illiterate, yet she seemed to know the details and wording of the recently passed statement on human rights. He asked, with a low voice, "Bett, how do you know of these matters?" "Why, by keepin' still and mindin' things," she replied.

This conservative young lawyer had no ax to grind concerning slavery, but Bett's argument that afternoon was so compelling and reasonable that he knew she had a good case. He had, after all, been one of the writers of the very declaration she had cited, and he wondered how it would stand up in court under the question of slavery. He agreed to take Bett's case, putting the principles of

Elizabeth "Mumbet" Freeman. Watercolor on ivory
by Susan Anne Livingston Ridley Sedgwick, 1811.

the declaration to the test in court. Ultimately, the declaration would also test its co-authors, including John Ashley himself.

Bett, who later took the name Elizabeth Freeman, was born around 1744 to native African parents. At a relatively young age, she and her sister Lizzie were purchased at a slave market in Albany, New York. They became the personal slaves of Hannah Ashley, the Dutch wife of John Ashley. Bett was considered an indispensable servant to Hannah, always focused and on-task. Those who knew Bett said that she often pitched in when her sister could not—or would not—finish her own tedious work, to prevent Lizzie from being punished.

Hannah Ashley's attitude toward her slaves followed the doctrines of the Dutch Reformed Church, which considered owning slaves a divine right. She was known as a cruel mistress and was heartily disliked by the servants. Mr. Ashley's views were far different, stemming from his English upbringing in the Congregational Church. His theory of slavery was based on the Book of Exodus in the Bible, which required seven years of service, and then freedom was granted—much like the guidelines for an indentured servant. Hannah was a formidable woman, and the husband and wife's opposing views created a good deal of tension in the household.

One of Bett's primary jobs in the evenings was to sit outside the home's study and fetch drinks for the men gathered about the fire there. Long hours she spent quietly doing her mending and listening to the heated discussions from the next room, as important politicians from the Berkshires came together to consider brewing independent riots in Boston. One night Bett overheard Ashley and his new friend Sedgwick, thirty-seven years Ashley's junior and educated at Yale University, fuming over the recent circulations by Samuel Adams and debating town and county issues. Bett tended the fire and listened carefully to their conversations when their voices became low. Bett's vocabulary and rhetoric grew, and her intellectual mind was offered much food for thought.

During January 1773 Bett spent a great deal of time tending to the fire in the upstairs study while a group of eleven men pondered their task: They had been appointed by the Town Meeting of Sheffield to "take into consideration the grievances which Americans in general and Inhabitants of this Province in particular labor under." It was then that Bett began to hear the words and ideas that fired her spirit and impending lawsuit. Known as the "Sheffield Declaration," these men laid out in their debates this statement:

> That Mankind in a state of nature are equal, free, and independent of each other, and have a right to the undisturbed enjoyment of there [sic] Lives, there [sic] Liberty and Property . . . (and) that the great end of political society is to secure in a more effectual manner those Rights and privileges wherewith God and Nature have made us free

Bett began to realize the implications of these words. On the final night of debates, she held her breath as they sounded out the wording for the final declaration. As she refilled the rum cups, she could not help but smile as she saw the clerk diligently writing the words in black ink. The room was full of white men who nodded approvingly at what she knew in her heart was the foundation of her freedom and the future of her brothers and sisters. It was then that she knew she had allies, despite their differences, and that these men would stand by these principles they believed in so strongly.

Late into that night, as she finished up Lizzie's ironing with the last of the coals from the study's fire, Bett's mind raced. The words "equal, free, and independent" rang like bells, and she embraced her work with the knowledge that it was finite. Silently she repeated to herself each word she could remember, etching the memory of the vital clauses deeper in her mind.

For eight years Bett continued to work in silence with her sister and the other household slaves under Hannah's command. During this time Sedgwick and Ashley continued their discussions and friendship, while Bett attended them closely. The two friends drank together the night the Massachusetts Constitution of 1780 was ratified, and raised a glass to their immense contribution. Bett kept track of the political climate and by this time was well versed in the law. She had at her disposal a "classroom" filled with experience and experiments—all with the comfort of a voyeur.

It was on a day in February 1781 that Bett decided she had put up with enough. Her sister Lizzie had made her mistress very angry, and when Bett ran into the room to see what the shouting was about, she saw Hannah going for the fire iron. Bett jumped in front of her sister to protect her and took the blow from the red-hot poker in her arm. She left the Ashley household that day, refusing to return. It was then that Bett sought the help of Theodore Sedgwick, confident that her knowledge and interpretation of the law was correct. Although she knew him to be a conservative—downright intolerant of the lower classes—she also understood the power and conviction of legal rights. Her debating skills had been developed over the years by listening to Sedgwick and his colleagues, and he was compelled to consider her case.

When Sedgwick decided to take the case and help Bett, it meant suing his friend John Ashley for Bett's freedom as well as damages. Ironically, Ashley himself silently sided with Sedgwick and Bett in the case. This was his chance to finally challenge his wife's cruel actions, but more importantly it was an opportunity to find out how the Declaration of Rights would apply to the question of slavery. Ashley resigned from his position of judge, retained his own lawyers, and quietly cheered the opposing team.

Bett's stand in court itself was remarkable. At that time a woman could only be a party to a *criminal* case. She could not stand alone in court as a plaintiff in a *civil* suit. So, another of Ashley's servants—one named Brom—was added as a plaintiff. On May 28, 1781, the Berkshire County Court of Common Pleas in Great Barrington heard the personal writ of replevin—one used to recover personal property—in *Brom & Bett vs. J. Ashley Esq.* In this case the "property" was the two plaintiffs themselves.

John Ashley had to give up his seat as judge in order to play defendant. He hired David Noble and Jonathan Canfield as his counsel, and Sedgwick hired Tapping Reeve—the founder of the first law school in the United States—to work alongside him on behalf of the antislavery movement. Ashley's lawyers did not give up without a fight, since all the men ultimately wanted to test the strength of their declaration.

Bett's argument hinged upon Article I of the Declaration of Rights in the Massachusetts Constitution of 1780, which was similar to those of the Sheffield Declaration. The passage began with the statement that "All men are born free and equal, and have certain natural, essential, and unalienable rights." In front of the court, she articulately reasoned that she was "not a dumb beast, but of mankind," and therefore this equality and freedom should apply to her as it did to all persons.

Sedgwick's goal was that his argument would prove that the new constitution waived any previous assumptions made by the "purchase" of his plaintiffs. The defense stood firm that his client had bought the slaves and therefore owned them as his property. Sedgwick made the case that the issue of buying and holding slaves had never been governed and that the new constitution now made the practice contrary to basic human rights. As a result, he argued, his clients should have their property (their freedom) returned and be compensated for the lapse in this breach of rights.

The court came to its decision: ". . . in this case the jury find that the aforesaid Brom & Bett are not and were not at the time of the purchase of the original writ the legal negro servants of him the said John Ashley during their life . . . and that the said Brom & Bett do recover against the said John Ashley the sum of thirty shillings lawful silver Money, Damages, and the Costs of this suit Paned at five pounds fourteen shillings and four pence like Money and hereof the s. Brom & Bett may have their Executions."

The judge went on to say that Ashley had the right to appeal to a higher court if he wished. To sufficiently test his theories, the defendant did take his case to the Massachusetts Supreme Judicial Court, where the decision of the lower court was upheld. Ultimately, the only party left upset by the outcome was the bitter Hannah Ashley.

Bett, who took the name Elizabeth Freeman in celebration of her new status, was the first slave to be set free in Massachusetts. This case was not just a trial for personal freedom, however, since it served as a constitutional model. Bett was fully aware that the court's decision would allow others to follow in her footsteps and gain their own freedom.

Since she had sued on principle of human rights instead of abuse (as her wound would have warranted), Bett changed the face of slavery in the courtroom. The highest court in Massachusetts had declared that slavery was an unconstitutional practice, and thus Massachusetts stood at the political forefront of a growing nation looking for guidance. The money received in compensation from the lawsuit was split between the plaintiffs. Bett chose to buy a piece of land and a house, a wise and unheard of investment for even a white woman in those days, let alone a black woman. Her reputation spread far and wide.

Bett certainly knew of Ashley's continued ties with Sedgwick and his antislavery sentiment during and after the trial. She refused, though, to return to the Ashley household as a paid servant, certainly not as a slight to Mr. Ashley but as a result of her dislike for Hannah and the treatment she and her sister received at her hand.

Instead, Bett chose employment with the Sedgwick family as a servant, nurse, and midwife. Her bond with Catherine, the mistress of the house, was very strong. Bett cared for the elderly Pamela, Catherine's mother, at a time when many disregarded the senile; but Bett took the time to treat her as an equal even when Pamela was in her weakest mental state. Bett embraced the family and its members as if they were her own and was treated with the same kind of respect. This relationship is testament to Bett's warm personality and intellect. Theodore Sedgwick and his relatives were far from liberal, and were known to look on the common people with great disdain. His respect for Bett, however, was deep and profound.

Bett was also known for her good company. Guests at the Sedgwick home would often seek her counsel and conversation. She was well respected and known not only for her traditional female roles as midwife and nurse but also for her keen insights into the current political climate.

Bett's death in 1829 at the age of eighty-five was devastating to Catherine, who decided to personally write her epitaph. She also chose to have Bett, who had been nicknamed "Mumbet" by the family, buried in the family plot, a decision which created quite a stir. The burial ground, affectionately known as "The Sedgwick Pie" for its round shape, had never had a non-blood relative buried there— and never has since. The grave marker for Mumbet still stands today at Center Cemetery in Stockbridge, next to Catherine's own:

ELIZABETH FREEMAN
Known by the name of MUMBET.
Died Dec 28 1829. Her supposed age was 85
years. She was born a slave and remained a slave

for nearly thirty years. She could neither read nor
write, yet in her own sphere, she had no superior
or equal. She neither wasted time nor property.
She never violated a trust, nor failed to perform a
duty. In every situation of domestic trial, she was
the most efficient helper, and the tenderest friend.
Good mother, farewell.

ABIGAIL ADAMS
1744–1818

A Founding Mother

*B*y their eighteenth wedding anniversary, Abigail had reached her limit of grief and depression and sat down to write John a letter that bared her soul. "Who shall give me back Time? Who shall compensate to me those years I cannot recall?" she asked him, adding that she might have had more happiness if her husband were less wise. Their separation was pulling her down, and after so many years of managing the farm and businesses alone, she longed for the simpler days of their youth. Abigail had always prided herself in how she supported the public work of her husband, but she was tiring of taking care of everything on the home front. Most of all, she was lonely.

Local gossip began to question John's devotion to her, and although she knew that he loved her, years of separation had taken a toll on Abigail's confidence. But John's letters revived her spirits with sentiments matching her own. "What a fine affair if we could flit across the Atlantic as they say the Angels do from Planet to Planet," he wrote.

Abigail was the second of four children, born in 1744 to the Reverend William and Elizabeth Smith of Weymouth. Her father, a Harvard graduate, ministered in the town for forty-nine years. Along with her sisters, Abigail was taught reading and writing in order to study the Bible. William Smith knew the value of education, so his daughters also learned arithmetic and other basic skills. Although there were no schools for girls that equaled those for boys, Reverend Smith strongly encouraged his daughters to use his extensive library to educate themselves. Abigail's mother kept a well-run house and raised her daughters with impeccable housekeeping skills.

Abigail was known as the stubborn one of the family. She was socially distant from other children in the town because of her father's ministry, so most of her close friendships developed when she was away visiting her Grandmother Quincy or Uncle Tufts in Boston. As Abigail reached her teens, she began to exchange letters with these friends, referring to herself as "Diana," after the Roman goddess. Her friends followed suit, adopting pen names like "Calliope" and "Myra." They gave similar names to their beaus, naming John Adams—Abigail's future husband—"Lysander" (from Shakespeare's *A Midsummer Night's Dream*.)

"Lysander" first appeared in the Smith household with his friend John Cranch, who was actively seeking Abigail's older sister's hand in marriage. Abigail looked up to her sister's well-educated suitor and engaged him in lengthy conversations about literature. He encouraged her to read John Milton and Alexander Pope and corresponded with her about them and other authors. He also began to tutor her in French. His friend John Adams was intrigued by this young woman's intelligence and thirst for knowledge, and soon he, too, began bringing her books and corresponding with her.

John's and Abigail's temperaments were enough alike that at first Abigail did not care for the stubborn, short-tempered lawyer. But she soon softened her opinion, and they became engaged. It was to be a long engagement, during which time they wrote to each

Abigail Smith Adams

other often, using their pen names Diana and Lysander. Abigail and John were married in Weymouth on October 25, 1764. Abigail was nineteen years old, her husband ten years her senior.

The young couple moved to a ten-acre farm next to John's mother's home in Braintree, about 5 miles from Abigail's hometown. Abigail gave birth to a girl, named Abigail, in July 1765. Almost exactly two years later, their son John Quincy was born. Abigail took her job as a mother very seriously, reading John Locke's theories on child rearing and preparing herbal remedies for her children to improve their health. She was also heavily influenced by James Fordyce (author of *Sermons for Young Women, 1766*), whose "rationalist" sermons about raising children charged mothers with the responsibility to form children by their own good example.

During these first years of marriage, John became involved in local politics. Already he felt torn between the financial steadiness of his law practice and his sense of duty and the excitement of political life. He was elected a town selectman, and joined the Sons of Liberty Monday Night Club, an early revolutionary society.

John was not the only one deeply interested in politics. Abigail studied history and found these pre-revolutionary times very exciting. Her very close friend was Mercy Otis Warren, whom Abigail respected for both her talents as a mother and her strong voice as a political satirist (using a male pen name). John was equally impressed by Mercy's sharp wit and keen observations of the current political climate. Abigail also wrote often to their English friend Catherine Macaulay, who was sympathetic to the American cause. Abigail liked to embellish details of the stresses of English oppression when writing to this friend overseas.

Abigail and her circle of friends had a keen sense of the history that was being made in their own time. She felt strongly enough about her political convictions to encourage her husband to quit his private practice as a lawyer and follow his sense of duty to join Congress in Philadelphia. This meant hard times financially for their budding family and a great deal of separation for her and her husband, yet Abigail had confidence that John was participating in something too important to be held back by her selfishness. In a letter to Mercy after John had announced a second term in Congress, Abigail acknowledged John's need to be a part of the new government: "I found his honour and reputation much dearer to me, than my own present pleasure and happiness, and I could by no means consent to his resigning at present, as I was fully convinced he would suffer if he quitted."

Throughout their time apart, John always encouraged Abigail's political interest and enjoyed her input, just as he encouraged Mercy Warren to write and publish her political satire. John consistently relied on Abigail's letters from home as the most reliable source of information and news concerning the battles and political happenings in the Boston area. John was impressed and moved by his wife's writing; he did not feel he was nearly as eloquent as Abigail. John often showed her letters to other members of Congress, even quoting from a letter in a speech to that assembly. Abigail was embarrassed by this and asked him to burn her letters; she was conscious of her lack of formal education and felt unworthy of such an honor.

In addition to writing about day-to-day events, Abigail shared her opinions with John. In perhaps her most famous letter, she reminded John about the true meaning of equal rights and representation: "I desire you would remember the ladies, and be more generous and favourable to them than your ancestors." She asked that lawmakers not give unlimited power to husbands, suggesting that "all Men would be tyrants if they could," and warning that women might begin a rebellion of their own if they had no voice in the laws. Not many women of her time would have dared suggest that her husband was overlooking something in his logic, especially when it challenged conventions.

As a feminist, she pointed out the hypocrisy of even those politicians with whom she generally agreed. In a May 1776 letter she reminded John that he and his colleagues were fighting for equality while happily controlling their wives. Her letters were at times heated and passionate, and she was never frightened of negative repercussions of her bold ideas. John was more concerned about the opinion of those beyond her close friends when it came to defying conventions. When he learned that she was teaching Latin to their daughter Nabby, he cautioned her not to tell many people, since it was "scarcely reputable" for girls to understand Latin.

Human equality was a core issue to Abigail, and not just equal rights for women. Slavery distressed her, since it seemed contradictory to independence. Because of this she did not trust the patriotism of southern states where the economy so heavily depended on slavery. She expressed this best in a letter to John, warning that he should look at the commitment level of those who had no problem enslaving other humans.

Letters between Braintree and Philadelphia took about two weeks to arrive, making conversations difficult for the couple to follow. John's letters were carried the 300 miles by his personal messenger rather than a letter carrier because they were often filled with descriptions of confidential congressional deliberations as well as his own frustrations.

In late 1776 during a short visit home, John and Abigail conceived another child. While he sat in Congress in Baltimore, Abigail gave birth to a stillborn girl. She also sat alone through her mother's fatal dysentery, and the death of a close friend and servant. She was beginning to feel deeply the strain of her loneliness but weathered it with the attitude that this was her form of public service.

In early 1778 John left for Europe, where he pled the American cause for independence in hopes of foreign support. He took their ten-year-old son John Quincy with him. While Abigail worried about her son and husband making the arduous winter journey across the Atlantic Ocean to France, she was busy with the household business. Up until John's European tour, she had double-checked almost every financial and family decision with him. In 1778, with long delays in international mail delivery, she had to make these decisions herself. Now Abigail was writing to tell John about a real-estate investment or business move she had made, instead of asking for his opinion. Although she stayed home in Braintree, Abigail was recognized as the wife of the French Ambassador, and French naval officers often visited and invited her to dine on their ship.

It was a year and a half—August 1779—before John finally came home. Abigail was heartbroken again three months later when he was sent back to France. This time he took both their sons, John Quincy and Charles. John's personal sacrifices were clearly rewarded with recognition, but Abigail's were not, and his prolonged absences doubled her own responsibilities. Although deeply upset, she concluded that manipulating him to stay home and lead a life that would always leave him wondering "what-if" would only leave them both miserable for the rest of their lives. If she let him follow his dreams, she could be a part of something important and have the hope of a quiet and content future with her beloved husband.

So Abigail kept focused, setting her mind to domestic affairs and her new import business. She had noticed that the small gifts John sent from France, while inexpensive there, would have cost dearly in the states, if available at all. Thus, once John arrived in Bordeaux to serve his second term, he sent her packages of glassware, silk scarves, gloves, and other goods, which she sold to supplement her income. As she got a better idea of what people wanted, she began telling John exactly what to purchase. He finally suggested that she write directly to the overseas merchants themselves. She did, and was soon trading and selling, hiring Mercy Warren and her Uncle Isaac in Boston to handle distribution of the goods. Abigail invested the profits in real estate and began to rent property. She was able to manage during John's absence with the silver coins that he had left and the income from her import business. She also made a decent profit renting some of their land and houses to tenants who took care of the properties. All the while Abigail kept a watchful eye on the political situation and made it a priority to ensure that John's political reputation remained intact. She was the first to jump on any sign of political mischief behind his back.

News from Europe, always seriously delayed, was distressing. John Quincy had traveled to St. Petersburg with an inexperienced diplomat, and Charles was on his way home alone by ship, a terrible voyage that took more than six months. Abigail was beside herself. When he finally got home, Charles told her that John had been very sick when he left. Letters were long in coming.

During the winter of 1781–1782, Abigail fell into a depression, which deepened in March with the news that John was staying on in Europe for another term. She became bitter that his years of public service were not paying off, and that people around her were prospering while she struggled alone. She felt that the people John was working for did not deserve his service, and that he should come home and make more money in private practice.

Abigail finally began to consider joining John in Europe and decided to use the excuse of "wifely duty" to persuade him to let her make the arduous journey across the Atlantic. At the same time John once again wrote of resigning and coming home, but then he dragged his feet, hoping for an appointment to a new

European position. The ambassador was severely torn, and his frequent letters told Abigail opposing things.

Finally, in autumn 1783, John sent for Abigail and their daughter Nabby to come to Europe, but Abigail was hesitant to make the winter crossing. She pleaded with him to return home and told him she was beginning to wonder if he loved politics more than her. Then Abigail's father died, and she was left to deal with that blow alone. By January, however, she was making travel plans. After a great deal of procrastination and waiting for a possible letter that John had changed his mind, mother and daughter set sail in May, a month after John expected them to arrive in London.

The voyage was worse than she expected, but once the initial bout of seasickness was over, Abigail took it upon herself to clean up the ship and teach the cook how to do his job. She began a journal to keep track of the days and record her trip. A storm, followed by an equally harrowing calm spell during which neither the water nor the air moved for days, prompted Abigail to reflect, in what might be a metaphor for her own life. She realized a life of excitement and turbulence was far more interesting than a sedentary life, like the still waters around the ship.

After four weeks, the captain finally spotted land, and the passengers were soon safely ashore. Abigail spent three weeks in London before John came to meet his family, then they made the trip to France together. This was the first time in more than four years that Abigail had seen her husband.

She was fascinated with the differences between her New England world and England, but her with Puritan attitudes she could not approve of the excesses of London aristocracy. Much to her dismay, she was forced to purchase dresses in the local style so she could fit in with other diplomats and their wives at social functions. Her disapproval increased when they reached Paris. She wrote after arriving, "It is the dirtyest place I ever saw."

Abigail found Paris cramped and thought that the houses were ugly and disorganized. They chose a house in Auteuil, a suburb far enough away from the stink and bustle of inner Paris. Even here, Abigail had to deal with local tradition, including servants with specialties, each of whom would do only one or two designated tasks. After hiring eight French servants, whom she referred to as a "pack of Lazy wretches," Abigail found herself again shopping for dresses to fit in with the new image she had to uphold. These expenses, plus the rent on their thirty-room home and the cost of entertaining droves of diplomats, took a toll on the sensibility of the frugal woman.

Local customs were just as difficult for Abigail to get used to as the high prices. She was appalled at the way women kissed men in greeting and was dismayed by the seeming lack of work ethic among the masses. Sundays unsettled her, since the French used the day to let go and relax with drinking, song, and festivals instead of spending it in Puritan reverence. Only by the end of her stay in Auteuil had Abigail finally come to a moderate acceptance of her surroundings.

After some trepidation, John accepted the post as Ambassador to England. Finding a house there proved difficult and expensive, but the Adamses finally found a much smaller residence than they had in France. Abigail found everything in London overpriced, which again sorely tried her New England thrift. Despite this, Abigail liked England much more than France.

While in London the Adamses were required to keep up appearances with a busy social life, far from Abigail's favorite job. She recalled in letters to friends back home the ordeal of standing for four hours in a stuffy hall just to meet the King and the royal family, none of whom impressed her. She described the King as red-faced but polite, and the Queen and her daughters as unpleasant and "very plain, ill shaped and ugly."

Particularly hard for the couple was complying with the social requirements on John's American salary. It was far too low to pay for the social life expected of a public official, by English standards. Newspapers were cruel to the ambassador and his family, criticizing Americans for being cheap and unable to keep up to proper standards. Because of this, the Adamses favored a close circle of American friends and those English who had supported American freedom, remaining rather private in their social lives.

Attempting to keep abreast of events at home, Abigail invited every American ship captain to dinner at her home in Grosvenor Square. The news in 1786 was increasingly discouraging. The American economy was failing miserably, and Abigail was displeased by the news of Shays's Rebellion: Instead of applauding the New England farmers for standing up for positive political change, she saw the rebellion as destructive to the young government. Her impressions of American culture were being influenced by her time in London, despite her strong desire to stay connected to her homeland. Abigail's political views began to look much more conservative now that her government was established. She believed in order and hierarchy, which she deemed indispensable in a stable society.

When, in May 1788, Abigail and her family finally moved back to Braintree, Abigail was certain that their time in the public spotlight was over. But John's former colleagues had different plans for the Adamses. The time was at hand to elect the new republic's first president and vice president, and John was the favorite for vice president. He was elected in the fall of 1788, and the Adams family became second only to George and Martha Washington. The Adamses moved to New York, at that time the capital, and John began his first term as vice president.

Abigail was by now supportive of John's political life since it was not separating them and she could have a front-row seat at her favorite event: politics. Being "Second Lady," though, was not without its drawbacks. Abigail missed her children, who were spread across the East in school and with their own families, and the demanding social schedule left no personal time for her and John. The change of the capital to Philadelphia meant another stressful and expensive move. John, meanwhile, found his position boring with very little but social appearances to occupy him.

Despite the downside of the vice presidency, John and Abigail did not want to lose to a challenger in the next election, so they accepted Washington's invitation to a second term. Abigail's political role and opinions, though, began to take a toll on her relationships. Her status and lack of time kept her isolated from friends, and the increasingly polarizing political debates of the times were separating her and John from their colleagues from the Revolution. Abigail's greatest loss was of her friend, Mercy Warren: Abigail had no tolerance for differing opinions and, convinced that Mercy was just plain wrong, refused to befriend her any longer.

During John's second term Abigail remained at their home in Braintree (now named Quincy). While in New York she had contracted malaria and was frequently plagued by it, sometimes for months at a time. Yellow fever was rampant in Philadelphia, killing one tenth of its population in one epidemic alone, and she was thought safer at home. John spent as much time with her as possible, returning home during the long congressional recesses. This arrangement was financially better, since without a full household in the capital, John was spared the expenses of entertaining. Even then, the couple missed each other severely and neither liked the arrangement.

Despite Abigail's growing conservatism, she kept her liberal beliefs about women's rights to education, eagerly reading publications such as "Bennett's Strictures on Female Education" and "Vindication of the Rights of Women" by Mary Wollstonecraft.

Although some of these ideas went too far for Abigail, she agreed with the most controversial principle—that women were intellectual equals to men. Strangely enough, her liberal ideas about equality did not translate into social settings. Abigail was still quite convinced that the average person in the lower class was incapable of understanding government and would blindly follow those who said what they wanted to hear. She believed that all decisions should be made by those who were in office, and she feared that too much control given to the masses would cause constant disruption and instability.

Near the end of Washington's second term as president, he announced to his close circle of friends that he planned to retire. This left Abigail and John debating once again their level of commitment to political life. Abigail missed her husband a great deal and was not sure if she was physically or socially up to being the graceful Mrs. Washington's successor. Despite her apprehensions and complaints, Abigail believed that John was the best man to fill the role of president.

In December 1796 John Adams was elected president, with Thomas Jefferson as his vice president. As before, no official residence was provided, and Abigail once again had to manage all the details of their farms while worrying about the move to Philadelphia. No longer could she duck out of the immense social responsibilities, for as First Lady she would have the constant job of hostess. For several months after John had gone ahead to Philadelphia, Abigail stayed behind and took care of negotiating with tenants and finding a caretaker for their home. John wrote constantly, begging her to drop everything and join him.

The Adamses took over the Washingtons' residence, which was in a sorry state; John did not do well managing it during Abigail's absence. So Abigail, with her skill for housekeeping, went straight to organizing the new home. Once settled, she established a strict daily routine as First Lady. She rose at 5:00 A.M. and had the next three hours to herself—the only personal time she enjoyed. At 8:00 A.M. breakfast was served and the day's fast pace began. By 11:00 A.M. she was preparing for the throngs of visitors and guests that would call in the afternoon. Following that she returned official visits. Some days were entirely devoted to planning large dinner parties for the cabinet and other government officials. The family had very little time to spend at their Quincy home during summers, as they had hoped. And then tragedy struck, soon after the move to Washington, when Abigail and John's once-successful son Charles died of liver failure. It had been no secret to Abigail and John that Charles's health was deteriorating from his inability to control his drinking. He had been ill with this addiction for years, and although not a surprise, his death was still heartbreaking to his family.

During John's presidency the new capital city was just taking shape. Washington was barely habitable when the Adamses first moved into the presidential mansion during the chilly November of 1800. Unfinished roads were dangerous and there was far too little housing to accommodate all of the government officials moving into town. Abigail complained frequently that the new executive mansion was drafty and its unfinished rooms not nearly ready for guests. Abigail also lamented over the slow pace of southern life and the slave-owning culture that was still active in the area. She was frustrated with the lack of incentive of even the poorest of white men, who would not do a job no matter the pay if they felt it was not fit for a person of their race.

Abigail was a very influential First Lady, which was noted by many during John's presidency. Office-seekers often approached her to gain the president's attention. Her influence stemmed from John's implicit trust in her judgment, a beacon for him in the shady world of politics. At times they were criticized for this closeness, opponents suggesting that John was unable to make any decision without her approval. Abigail and John frequently referred to themselves as though they were one person, and they grew much closer during this time.

But their stay in Washington was short-lived. In December 1800 Thomas Jefferson was elected president. Although sore over the loss and feeling let down by the American public, Abigail was happy to settle back into her old life in Quincy. She left Washington in February, and John left quietly early on the morning of his successor's inauguration day. Abigail was sure that the country would fall apart without her husband and was fretful over their future finances without John's salary, but she was happy to leave nonetheless.

The following years at the Quincy home helped Abigail relax on many of her political views now that she did not take them so personally. She had a constant flow of family members visiting, as well as plenty of her own children and grandchildren living with her. John Quincy was elected senator in 1803, and in the summer of 1805 Abigail had almost the entire family under her roof. Even Nabby visited that summer with her children. True to form, Abigail ran the household and the farm and enjoyed the luxury of having her family near.

Family issues continued to arise, however, including Abigail's constant influence over John Quincy's children and the friction this caused between her and his wife, Louisa. As always, Abigail did not hold back on her advice, which was less than welcome. Nabby's husband, with whom she had had difficulties in the past, was arrested and went to jail, after which the family moved to central New York to begin life anew. Just a few years later Nabby underwent risky surgery for breast cancer; she survived, only to die from a recurrence of the disease.

Abigail watched nearly all her best friends and all her brothers and sisters die. Perhaps realizing her own mortality, she began to repair old friendships with those she had turned away from for holding opposing beliefs. One of the most important relationships she rebuilt was that with Mercy Warren, who died just four years after their reconciliation. Abigail also took time to repair the bond with Thomas Jefferson, a man whose presidency she cursed and with whom she had argued actively since their many disagreements during the Adamses' years abroad.

Abigail was proud to see her son John Quincy appointed to his father's old post, ambassador to Britain at the end of the War of 1812. Even when he was overseas, Abigail continued to meddle with his affairs, writing to the president about changing John Quincy's post and salary. She missed him and her grandchildren terribly, however, and was overjoyed to see his entire family at her home in August 1817. Abigail was especially pleased to be left with the charge of her grandchildren while John Quincy and Louisa went on to Washington when he became secretary of state. Abigail reveled in Louisa's request for advice on being the proper wife of a political figure, and the two began to mend their rocky relationship.

Only two months after John Quincy and Louisa's return home, Abigail was stricken with typhoid fever. It progressed quickly, and she died on October 28, 1818. John, although crushed by his loss, had a serenity about him as he reflected on the fullness of her life and the undeniable quality of their fifty-four years together. John survived Abigail by seven and a half years, during which time he enjoyed good health. He lived through the first two years of John Quincy's presidency. Ironically, on the fiftieth anniversary of the Declaration of Independence—July 4, 1826—both he and his friend Thomas Jefferson died.

History has been blessed by Abigail's—and the entire Adams family's—legacy of letter writing, which has kept their story and the details of their times alive.

· · ·

Adams National Historic Site in Quincy includes the home of four generations of the Adams family. The house is filled with family possessions that give a clear picture of Abigail's life and times. It was she who saw to the addition of the house's most recent wing.

DEBORAH SAMSON

1760–1827

"Official Heroine of the Commonwealth of Massachusetts"

$\mathcal{D}$eborah could hear the hum of the crowd from her perch on the short stool behind the curtain at Providence Hall. Drawing in a deep breath, she let it out with a silent chuckle, recalling the comments she heard as she had tried to sneak in through the building's side entrance. Audience members who had spotted her whispered and exclaimed in half-muted voices, "Could this be the one? Why, it seems like a lad, all of age eighteen!" Perhaps, she thought, she should not have worn her costume into the performance hall, yet the sensation that it created filled her with even more glee.

Her mind wandered back to the very first time she wore a man's outfit, which had made everyone so upset. Again, she giggled, as she remembered the dipped brow of Master Thomas as the congregation threatened to have her excommunicated for such indecency.

She recalled those first few hours on the road, walking toward Uxbridge in a uniform that she had crafted herself, how scared and

Engraving of Deborah Samson, the frontispiece from Herman Mann's
The Female Review: or, Memoirs of an American
Young Lady, *1797*

thrilled and positively uncertain she was about the chance she was about to take. One thing she knew she would never forget was that last moment before she entered the tent, risking her reputation in search of adventure and a life of action, when she stood almost frozen in youthful anticipation. There she paused, getting ready to enlist in the Fourth Massachusetts Regiment as Robert Shurtleff. *I felt like I was standing on the plank, unsure if it was sharks or warm waters which awaited me,* she thought. *I wish I could tell them that.*

Tucking her graying hair neatly up into her cap and straightening her pressed uniform, she stood and shook the haze of nostalgia from her mind, mentally rehearsing the opening lines of her speech.

Deborah Samson was the second of seven children born to Jonathan Samson and Deborah Bradford Samson of Plympton, Massachusetts. Her parents were married on October 17, 1751, and had their first child, Robert Shurtleff Samson, who died at the age of eight. Deborah was born on December 17, 1760, and was the oldest of six siblings—two girls and three boys who were born over the next five years. Her family was very poor despite the fact that they were descendants of the well-known second governor of Plymouth Colony, William Bradford, who arrived in America on the *Mayflower.*

Bathsheba LeBrocke was Deborah's grandmother, and it is said that this French lady spoiled Deborah when she came to visit. Bathsheba's influence on Deborah's future escapades was speculated upon by biographers Lucy Freeman and Alma Bond in their book *America's First Woman Warrior.* There they describe grandma Bathsheba telling fireside stories of Jeanne d'Arc and her fantastic crusades in men's garb, fighting for her cause at whatever price. As a young child Deborah cherished these heroic tales of defiance and bravery, as she did the stories of her father's cousin Captain Simeon Samson, who escaped from the enemy in the French and

Indian War by dressing as a woman. This same Captain Samson laughed at four-year-old Deborah when she asked if she could be his cabin boy. He told her "no" because she was a girl.

It seems that her father disappeared and was presumed dead, never to return, when Deborah was about five years old. Whether he actually died or just abandoned his large family is still debated by historians. Regardless, her mother was left with no option other than sending the children to live with relatives. First Deborah was sent to live with her mother's cousin, but this placement ended when her guardian died unexpectedly. From there she was forced into several foster-type homes before she finally ended up in the Thomas household in Middleborough. This arrangement has been described as a foster home by some historians and indentured servitude by others, but most likely it fell somewhere in between. The Thomas household was made up of Deacon Jeremiah Thomas (also recorded as Cephrus Thomas or Benjamin Thomas), his wife, and their eight sons. Even as the only girl out of nine children, Deborah was still required to do a great deal of the farm work, including working the fields, haying, milking the cows, and other hard labor.

During her stay at the Thomas's, Deborah often wore her foster brother's clothes to perform the outdoor work with greater comfort. During her spare time the boys were her playmates and friends; they taught her how to hunt and use a rifle, and she could run with the best of them. In the evenings, after her work was done, Deborah asked the boys to go over their schoolwork with her, which is how she learned to read, write, and do arithmetic. She had fewer duties in the winter months, which left her a little more time to spend studying. She eagerly listened to the animated conversations going on in Master Thomas's study about the brewing revolution. Her imagination already full of the tales she heard as a child, Deborah perched her chair as close to the door as she could.

She listened while weaving or doing her handwork, hearing all about the heroes in the making that were running about the countryside. Deacon Thomas was a patriot, and her own political beliefs were forming in this direction.

Once she turned eighteen and was technically freed from the legal bond to the Thomas family, Deborah decided to take on a new profession and taught school in Middleborough during the summers of 1779 and 1780. This work helped to support her independence for some time. She also took up work as a seamstress, weaving and sewing uniforms for the soldiers of the Continental Army. Although she was still living with the Thomas family, she was growing discontented with her situation and bored with watching the excitement of the Revolution go on around her without being able to participate.

In the spring of 1781 the twenty-one-year-old woman she put on a man's suit she had been working on and headed out to the town watering hole. Although she saw no harm in the charade, Deacon Thomas and the rest of the tight-knit conservatives in the town, who had just accepted her into the Baptist church, had much to say about her rebellious behavior. Threatening to excommunicate her and constantly berating her for this escapade, the community members added fuel to her discontent. She wanted to leave, to see other places, and to have the opportunity to start over. Considering her options, she determined that there was no way to travel alone as a woman, and that the only way to travel without money as a man was to join the army. She began to formulate her plan.

In May 1782 she finished up a well-tailored uniform to fit a man five foot seven inches, which happened to be her height. She placed it in a bag with a few other essential belongings, and on the morning of the 20th told Mrs. Thomas she was going out to look for work. Outside of town she changed into the uniform and walked the rest of the way to the tavern in Bellingham, where she signed up for a three-year term in the Fourth Massachusetts Regiment of the Continental Army under the name "Robert Shurtleff." She chose the name in honor of her brother who had died as a child. She enlisted as a resident of the town of Uxbridge to draw attention from her true identity. Soon the troops, including young, beardless Private Shurtleff, were headed for Worcester to join General George Washington.

She kept up the charade very well, even while lacking the facial hair to prove her testosterone level. The "other" men called her "Molly" because she didn't have to shave, and some called her "blooming boy." Not for a minute, however, did her fellow soldiers guess her disguise, and Private Shurtleff was always regarded as very brave and noted by "his" commanding officers as always being at the battle front.

Deborah served in Captain George Webb's Company and fought in many battles. Which battles, specifically, historians argue about, but most agree that she fought in the Tarrytown battle. At this battle she was slashed across the head with a saber and then shot in the thigh with a musket. Here again history has its disagreements—one story has it that Deborah extracted the bullet herself with a hunting knife, while another says that it remained in her leg until old age, causing her numerous health problems. Either way, she had to hide her injury in order to keep her sex a secret and never received proper medical attention.

At some point following Tarrytown, the young energetic private was assigned as an orderly to General John Patterson. It is during this time, as most sources have it, that troops were sent to Philadelphia to protect Congress during trouble in the fall of 1783. The city was having an outbreak of fever (some say typhoid), and when Private Shurtleff fell ill and unconscious "he" was taken to the hospital. In this state Deborah could hardly fend off an examination, and was quickly discovered by the doctor. In some stories she awoke at the crucial moment and pleaded with the physician, Dr. Barnabus Binney, to keep her charade a secret—in the name of patriotic duty—from the officers. Some legends have it that she was allowed to continue her escapades for quite some time after her discovery before the doctor broke down and wrote a letter to her commanding officer. But one thing is sure—the doctor was discreet in his disclosure.

As a result of being found out, Deborah was dismissed from the army. (One particularly nice story about her dismissal has her in the office of none other than General Washington himself, whereupon he quietly hands her a letter and some money and offers a few words of wisdom for the departing soldier, trying to spare her embarrassment.) Deborah traveled to West Point, New York, where she was honorably discharged on October 23. There are again historical rumors about her treatment, one of which includes a great deal of ridicule by her commanding officers before the official dismissal.

Her ruse exposed, Deborah's only option as a single woman was to return to family. Too ashamed to go see her mother, who was horrified at the scandal, she went to Stoughton to live with her aunt and uncle. Legend has it that she arrived in men's costume and actually pretended to be one of her other brothers for a period of time, continuing the cross-dressing to its fullest extent. Some say that she was still dressing like this when she met her future husband, Benjamin Gannett, and it was their meeting that coaxed her back into womanly attire. Whatever the case, it was not long after her arrival in Stoughton that she and Benjamin were married, in April 1784.

The Gannett family was fortunate to have three children of their own, Earl, Mary, and Patience, and adopted a fourth, Susanna Baker Shepard, despite financial difficulties. A few biographers, particularly those of the late nineteenth century, have been unkind to Benjamin Gannett because of his inability to provide riches for his family and because he, too, was not a war veteran. It is true that the large family lived in a three-room house in Sharon and had very little land to cultivate. It is also true that Deborah had health problems as a result of her war injuries. As time went on she was less able to do manual labor around the house, and her medical bills reached well over $600.

Paul Revere, who was as well known in his own day as he is now, lived close by in the town of Canton and found out about Deborah's financial problems. He visited the family, lending them $10, and quickly set things in motion to get a pension for Deborah. In 1804 Revere wrote a letter to W. Eustis, Esq., dated February 20, in support of her application, stating that "She is now much out of health. . . . They have a few acres of poor land which they cultivate, but they are really poor. She told me, she had no doubt that her ill health is in consequence of her being exposed when she did a Soldiers [sic] duty; and that while in the Army, she was wounded."

The biggest obstacle that Deborah faced in her pension application was that her virtue was constantly questioned; her sexual conduct was a major determining factor in whether or not she would get her pension. It was believed that no woman could have been in the company of men under wartime conditions and preserved her chastity. As if this weren't enough, her discharge papers had been lost, so the process took that much longer. Even John Hancock, the governor of the state, had stood up for Deborah and her alter-ego Private Shurtleff, writing a statement in a 1792 letter to D. Cobb of the pension board assuring him of her "extraordinary instance of female heroism by discharging the duties of a faithful gallant soldier, and at the same time preserving the virtue of Chastity of her Sex unsuspected and unblemished." This letter awarded her 34 pounds in a lump sum, but when Revere *and* Hancock joined forces along with her former commanding officer General John Patterson (now Judge Patterson of Congress), Deborah was finally granted a monthly benefit of $4.00 in November of 1783. Finally vindicating her time in the service, the Congressional Committee on Revolutionary Pensions stated that "the whole history of the American Revolution records no case like this, and furnishes no other similar example of female heroism, fidelity, and courage."

Around this time Deborah began her public life as a speaker. Two things motivated her decision to tell her story. She felt it was important to take an active role in persuading public opinion. Since her service was highly scrutinized after being discovered, Deborah wanted to do something to help her chances of increasing her pension and knew that public exposure would help. Deborah was also quite aware of the sensation she had caused and knew that she could capitalize on her infamy; her public speaking earned her family a much-needed income. She began to tour, giving stage performances and speeches about her time served in the war, for 25 cents admission. At forty-two, she was hardly a "lad" of eighteen, and her increasingly sore hip was a constant reminder of both her age and experience, yet she was eager to share her adventures with audiences across the East.

Deborah was in a delicate position, trying to display femininity and virtue while also proving without a doubt that she had really fought in the war. She felt it was most important to explain to the audience her reasoning behind joining the army, using universal themes that everyone could identify with. She proved to the audience her knowledge of the rifle, although sometimes in a great deal of pain, by performing the Manual of Arms. Deborah utilized the homes of the men who were once her commanding officers as lodging as she toured, not only to save money but to add another layer of credibility to her public image. Most convincing, however, was a constant incorporation of facts from the battlefield—details that only a soldier would know—into her performances.

In her "narration of facts," as she called it, the fully costumed soldier woman brought the audience into her world. Outlining the regiment's route of travel, she recounted her wounds in Tarrytown, and then the long march to Yorktown. Her great attention to detail and knowledge of facts left little doubt as to her participation in that battle: "Three successive weeks, after a long and rapid march, found me amidst this storm.—But, happy for AMERICA . . . when, on the delivery of Cornwallis's sword to the illustrious, the immortal WASHINGTON, or rather by his order, to the brave LINCOLN."

Deborah made it a point to speak in towns where her former officers and fellow soldiers lived, partly to show the public that she had nothing to hide in her story. She was graciously welcomed by them, and therefore found it much easier to be accepted into the communities. It was during her tour that she was able to reconnect with General John Patterson, who was essential in the granting of her pension. She toured all the way from Massachusetts to Rhode Island and New York, headlining at places like the Federal Theatre in Boston, the popular theatres of Worcester, and Park Theatre in New York City.

With her credibility as a soldier established, Deborah's most daunting task was to then prove her femininity and stand up for her decision to challenge prevailing gender roles. For this task she used a personal appeal, specifically reaching out to the women in her audience. She tried to unite the passion of patriotism with the fervor of her actions, taking the focus off her own personal rebellion and shifting it to the popular issue of every American's duty. In her speech she exclaimed, "Wrought upon at length, you may say, by an enthusiasm and phrenzy, that could brook no control—I burst the tyrant bands, which *held my sex in awe,* and clandestinely, or by stealth, grasped an opportunity, which custom and the world seemed to deny, as a natural priviledge."

This was as far as her political statements went, however. She did not take the opportunity to tout women's rights or encourage others to follow in her path; instead, she allowed her life to speak for itself. Deborah's presence on the stage was enough of a statement, defying conventions that discouraged women from being in entertainment. Although her story was developed from her own experiences, writer Herman Mann developed the script for her presentation and added a bit of the dramatic flair. She traveled alone during the entire tour and managed all of the business aspects, including promotion and all other areas of self-management. By the time the tour was over, Deborah made a profit of over $100, which was equivalent to several years' salary.

Deborah lived for many happy years with her son Earl and his wife, Mary, at their home in Sharon. At the age of sixty-six, she passed away in her home on April 29, 1827. Deborah's husband, Benjamin, continued to receive a small widower's pension from the government during the few remaining years of his life. His application for increased benefits was denied, yet their children did finally receive $466.66 from Congress a year after Benjamin's death in 1837, in compensation for Deborah's military service.

Deborah has the distinction of being the first woman to fight in the American Revolution, and also the first woman to join the lecture circuit. In 1983 she gained another "first" when she was declared the Official Heroine of the Commonwealth of Massachusetts by Governor Michael Dukakis on May 23. This was the first time any man or woman had been named as the official hero or heroine of a state in the history of the nation. Deborah Samson's unusual life neither changed popular opinion about women in the military nor began any movement for her gender, but the curiosity of her bold challenge captured the imaginations of so many.

• • •

Deborah Samson's original home in Plympton, though now privately owned, can be found on Elm Street. Sharon holds the most impressive amount of Samson memorabilia, including a statue of Deborah at the Sharon Public Library. Samson's last home still stands on East Street, and her gravesite can be found at nearby Rock Ridge Cemetery. A monument built in her honor by her grandson George Washington Gay is close by.

ELIZABETH PALMER PEABODY

1804–1894

Champion of Kindergartens

*T*he first day of school at Elizabeth and Mary Peabody's new kindergarten on Pinckney Street on Boston's fashionable Beacon Hill could not help but be a day of triumph for Elizabeth. For the past forty years she had championed the cause of early childhood education, and today, in 1859, the first public kindergarten in America opened its doors to welcome scrubbed and starched preschoolers.

Anyone else would have seen this as the crowning achievement of a long career. But so widespread were Elizabeth's interests and passions, and so intense her intellect, that even this culmination of a lifetime's work seemed to her more of a promising beginning than a mission accomplished. To Elizabeth, reaching a goal only put her in full stride toward the next one, and she would not rest until the kindergarten was accepted throughout American public education. There were teachers to train, school boards to convince, and parents to inspire. And there were other causes to promote.

Education—her own and others—had been central to Elizabeth's life since early childhood. She was born on May 16, 1804,

Elizabeth Palmer Peabody

in Billerica, Massachusetts, the first child of Nathaniel and Elizabeth (Palmer) Peabody. Her father, who made his living at various times as a doctor, dentist, and apothecary, was less of an influence in Elizabeth's life than was her mother, a teacher and herself a proponent of early childhood education.

Elizabeth's first experience with school was at age four, when she was thoroughly frustrated because she couldn't read as fluently as a six-year-old neighbor. She was the youngest student in her mother's school, and in this co-ed environment she would receive the same rigorous classical education as the Harvard-bound boys. Elizabeth thought deeply about religion, and by the time she was eleven she had already taken part in debates about subjects such as free will and original sin. The two themes—religion and education—would continue to dominate her life, and would become intertwined into a personal philosophy and mission.

It was when her parents moved the family to Lancaster, Massachusetts, in 1820 to try their hand at farming that Elizabeth, then sixteen, took over her mother's school. By then the Peabody family had grown to include Mary and Sophia, who would continue to play strong roles in Elizabeth's life, and three brothers: Nathaniel, George Francis, and Wellington. The latter two would die in their twenties, while Nathaniel would be financially dependent on Elizabeth for her entire life.

Elizabeth took her role as the eldest child very seriously, possibly because so much of the responsibility for the care of her siblings was thrust upon her. They were all her students in this first school, and when classes were over, she was still responsible for looking after them. When Sophia was twelve, Elizabeth, who was not living at home then, wrote her long letters, urging her to read, and assumed the job of her religious education. Elizabeth continued to advise her sister into adulthood, so much so that Sophia considered her meddlesome.

The responsibility that was put upon Elizabeth at an early age, coupled with her mother's passion for education, formed a character that valued intellect and duty to humanity above all. But in the process she never had a chance to grow up and mature at a normal rate. While her younger siblings played, she worked. The single-minded dedication to her work and to supporting her family was to shape her life in many ways.

It was in her first school in Lancaster that Elizabeth began to form and practice the principles that guided her teaching. She believed that education was the key to a successful and Christian life, and that with education and guidance, even the very young could distinguish right from wrong—and choose the former. So, to her, education was the key to social order as well as personal enrichment.

From the first, Elizabeth was a gifted teacher who could inspire students with her own enthusiasm for learning. Her teaching style was not the usual learning by rote that was practiced elsewhere in the early 1800s. Instead, Elizabeth taught through discussion, encouraging students to ask questions and to understand what they were learning. She stressed children's intellectual and spiritual growth, and used history as a platform from which to teach other subjects. These teaching methods were the same ones her mother had used, and they fit very well into Elizabeth's own goal of intertwining religious and spiritual growth with "book learning."

Rural life was not a success for the Peabody family. Elizabeth's father was not a good farmer, and her mother disliked being so far from the city and its social climate. So in 1822 the family moved to Salem, where Dr. Peabody would practice dentistry (much to Mrs. Peabody's chagrin, for she didn't think a dentist's wife was as socially elevated as a doctor's wife). And although Elizabeth's formal education ended at age sixteen when she took over the Lancaster school, she moved to Boston to earn money to send her younger brothers to Harvard.

Her mother's social aspirations and background were help-ful to Elizabeth as she began her life in Boston. The elder Eliz-abeth had always moved among the socially prominent, so Elizabeth was welcome in the best homes on Beacon Hill. She lived with distant relatives (as was proper for a single woman) and hobnobbed regularly with Harvard faculty and the intellec-tual leaders of Boston. It was from these families that she drew students for a new school.

Elizabeth opened her school at the corner of Mt. Vernon and Hancock Streets, convenient to those Beacon Hill homes. Unable to find good history books for young readers, Elizabeth wrote her own, and had her students copy it as their penmanship lessons. This was typical of her "just do it" attitude, and set her on another career path of writing and publishing.

While Elizabeth was teaching and writing her own textbooks, she was also busy learning. The same year that she opened the Boston school, while she was also studying French and German, she hired a Harvard student to teach her Greek. This was the begin-ning of a lifelong friendship and intellectual partnership; the Har-vard student was Ralph Waldo Emerson.

It was also during this time in Boston that Elizabeth met the prominent Unitarian preacher William Ellery Channing and began to study theology more deeply. Under Channing's guidance she found that the Unitarian ideals of human dignity and intellectual-ism fit her own thinking. She saw God as a loving parent, not the wrathful being portrayed by the more conservative Calvinists that had ruled the New England churches. She saw the natural order of the universe as proof of this view, and became a Unitarian even before there was an organized church.

While living and teaching in Boston fulfilled Elizabeth's intel-lectual needs, it did not meet her financial needs. Unable to recruit enough students for her school, she accepted a job in Maine as the teacher of a private school for a family and several of their neighbors' children. Her sister Mary, also a teacher, later joined her there.

While in Maine, Elizabeth had her first real romantic encounter. But long before that—as early as age fifteen—she realized that marriage was likely to put a halt to a woman's intellectual life. She also saw (or was convinced of it by her mother) that marriage meant submission, which was hardly the role she intended for herself. She refused her suitor, who later committed suicide.

In 1825 Mary and Elizabeth returned to the Boston area, living in Brookline, where Elizabeth could be nearer to Channing, who had become her mentor. She acted as his volunteer secretary, copying the notes for his sermons for publication. Even after they reopened the school in Boston the following year, both sisters spent their evenings with Channing and his wife, enjoying the lively conversation. When they opened their school, the Channings enrolled their daughter, helping the school gain prominence.

It was while Elizabeth and Mary kept school in Boston that they met Bronson Alcott. He was a progressive educator who came to Boston to spread his revolutionary theories: that children learned best without memorization or physical punishment, two sacred principles of traditional teaching. Elizabeth agreed wholeheartedly, finding Alcott's methods of teaching by discussion very similar to her own.

Private schools—both formal academies and the many schools taught in private homes—were far more open to new ideas than public schools. In a day when women were not considered worthy of academic studies, it was only in these schools that they could have a classical education. But it was difficult to get and keep enough students to make a living from these schools, and in 1831, the Peabody sisters closed their doors.

Elizabeth was deeply committed to education for women, and in the 1830s she became involved in adult programs, forming a class in 1833 to teach history and literature to twenty women. She also began holding adult conversations in the classics for women.

During this time both sisters lived at Mrs. Clarke's boarding house, as was usual for single people living in the city. There they met a young lawyer, who was also a member of the Massachusetts General Court (the state legislature). Horace Mann was recently widowed and still grieving deeply the loss of his wife. The two sisters became his friends and confidantes, helping him work through his loss.

The opinion of biographers is sharply divided as to whether Elizabeth was in love with Mann, but it is certain that they were very close. It is also certain that Mary was in love with him. But in 1833 Mary was sent by her family to accompany their younger sister Sophia to Cuba. Sophia was always considered fragile, and it was felt that a tropical climate would restore her health. Imagine Mary's distress at being sent so far away from the man she had come to love, especially when she was leaving him boarding in the same house as her sister. The situation was not helped by Elizabeth's detailed letters of every conversation she had with Mann in her sister's absence. She described all her efforts to pull him out of his sorrow: their long walks, their philosophical discussions, even his falling into her arms in tears. To Elizabeth, he was their joint mission, and she was simply keeping her sister informed and involved. But to Mary, these letters were growing proof that Elizabeth was taking her place. While Elizabeth's references to Mann were always in the role of a brother, Mary accused Elizabeth of acting improperly and hinted of harm to her reputation. This hurt Elizabeth deeply, both because she was devoted to Mary, and because as a teacher she was very conscious of her good reputation. Mary's jealousy was to drive the sisters apart for some time. Mary need not have worried, though, for it was Mary that Mann later proposed to and subsequently married.

Meanwhile, Elizabeth's adult classes and occasional writing were not paying her bills, so she made plans to open another school. Her reputation had grown and she found a location for her school, with a room where she could live. She was in the process of recruiting students for her new school when Bronson Alcott returned to Boston to open his own in 1834. A similar one he had begun in Pennsylvania had failed and he hoped that Boston's intellectual environment would be more receptive.

Typical of Elizabeth, she supported his efforts enthusiastically, turning all her own students over to him and helping him recruit more by introducing him to her prominent friends. Alcott furnished his new classroom lavishly, sparing no expense, although on borrowed money.

But for all his grand ideas about children's intuition and their ability to learn from experiences and stimulating discussion, Alcott was not prepared to teach anything substantive. So while his eighteen students enriched their minds through conversations with Alcott, ensconced in his custom-made, throne-like desk, it was Elizabeth who taught them the solid subjects of Latin, geography, history, and arithmetic.

She had agreed to work half days for him, spending her afternoons writing and earning a living. For this, Alcott promised to pay her $100 a quarter, far less than she would have made by teaching fewer students in her own school. But when the end of each quarter came, he had other more pressing debts—such as paying for the desk—and Elizabeth was never paid.

Meanwhile, she began spending her afternoons at the school, as well, at Alcott's request, to record his "conversations" with the students. She spent her evenings copying this journal for a book about Alcott's methods, *Record of a School*, published in 1835. Alcott got the notoriety and credit, but it was Elizabeth who paid for its publication.

By 1835 Elizabeth, still unpaid for her teaching, began having doubts about some of Alcott's methods. For one thing, he insisted that the students' journals be read aloud and discussed by the class, especially those parts that were the most introspective and revealing of their self-doubts. Elizabeth feared that this would create a competition among the students to see who could be the most self-doubting, in hopes of pleasing Alcott, who obviously prized this. She also worried about issues of confidentiality, since most of the children were under age ten. She did not agree with exposing a child's innermost thoughts to public scrutiny.

Elizabeth was then living in the same boarding house as the Alcotts, and dinner table conversation became more and more strained as her doubts about Alcott's methods increased. Relations worsened when Elizabeth discovered that Mrs. Alcott was reading her mail while she was at the school. When the second volume of *Record of a School* was nearing publication, Alcott decided to include the names of the children in the conversations. Elizabeth thought this a gross violation of their privacy and asked to have her name disassociated with the book. Finally, in 1836, Elizabeth left Boston and returned to live with her family, keeping up a lively correspondence with her Boston friends. Alcott was astonished that she had abandoned him.

And when the book eventually was published, without the disclaimer that Elizabeth had requested to separate her name from the content of the book, it caused such a furor that parents withdrew their children and Alcott's school closed. Yet instead of opening her own school and reclaiming the students, Elizabeth defended Alcott publicly, pointing out the merits in his teaching methods.

While living in Salem, Elizabeth renewed an old acquaintance with Lizzie Hawthorne, whose brother Nathaniel had written some short stories that Elizabeth liked. She took this shy writer under her wing, introducing him to publishers and important literary contacts that would further his career. She also introduced him to her frail sister Sophia, with whom he fell in love. Elizabeth's letters are far too circumspect to have mentioned if she herself had been hopeful of Hawthorne's attentions, but her biographers have speculated that perhaps once again she lost a man she loved to a sister.

Throughout the 1830s Elizabeth's intellectual and literary life flourished. Her friendship with the Emersons grew, and she was a regular member of Boston literary gatherings. Elizabeth was a bit of an anomaly, even in Boston, where women enjoyed far more intellectual freedom than elsewhere in the country. Unmarried women in her era were expected to be maiden aunts who lived off the kindness of relatives. They were not expected to be philosophers, religious thinkers, or leaders in education. They were also not expected to be in the public eye, and Elizabeth received more than a little attention for her exploits. Descriptions of Elizabeth in middle age tend to discuss her disheveled appearance, for she was disinterested in clothing. When given a new dress, she almost invariably gave it away to someone she felt was more in need. Her bonnets were crushed and worn askew, her hair in disarray. Elizabeth had more important things to think about than her appearance, as she championed one cause after another. By 1840, when she returned to Boston to open a bookshop at 13 West Street, Elizabeth was already known as a bit of an eccentric.

The West Street Bookshop, one of the most influential in America's literary history, was part book store and part lending library. Elizabeth imported foreign books and journals that had been unavailable to Boston readers, and the store served as a gathering place for the literati. Upstairs, Elizabeth's parents lived with her, as did both her sisters until they were married. The shop allowed Elizabeth to concentrate on teaching adults. It was well located, adjoining Washington Street, where Boston's publishing industry was centered, and it was only a block to Beacon Hill, where most of Boston's intelligentsia lived. These were people she already knew from family connections and from having taught their children. Liberal thinkers would patronize her shop for hard-to-find books, many of which Elizabeth printed in their first American editions. It is likely that Elizabeth was the first American woman to be a book publisher.

Along with being the meeting place for literate Bostonians, Elizabeth's bookshop became the headquarters for the Transcendentalists. In 1839 the shop became the venue for the famous "Conversations" by Margaret Fuller, a leading Transcendentalist. Two dozen women signed up for these conversations, where they not only heard new ideas but were urged to think for themselves. Elizabeth had long seen the connection between the Unitarians and the Transcendentalists, both of which recognized an unlimited potential of the human mind and spirit. But to many in Boston, Transcendentalism was atheism. Elizabeth made it her mission to show that the Transcendental movement was the natural union of liberal ideas with Christian doctrine. She viewed it as an example of the natural order, which brought her into ideological conflicts with the dogmatic Margaret Fuller. Fuller criticized Elizabeth, often personally and unkindly, but Elizabeth continued to support Fuller. Even when ill-used, as she had been by Alcott, Elizabeth was a generous woman without a trace of vindictiveness. The Transcendentalists had long tried to get their ideas into print, but had been largely snubbed by literary and intellectual publications. Elizabeth began the publication of *The Dial*, the journal of the Transcendental Club, with Margaret Fuller as its editor. In addition she published children's books by Nathaniel Hawthorne and an edition of his *Twice Told Tales*.

Elizabeth was also doing a lot of writing herself, much of which was published in *The Dial*. By the 1840s and 1850s, she had established the bookshop as a center for adult learning, with a series of history classes for women. During this time she also developed a set of charts to teach children history. Elizabeth not only published these tools and colored them by hand but also promoted their use tirelessly. She traveled all over the country showing them to schools.

These years were ones of change for Elizabeth's entire family. From living together at the bookstore, they began to separate. Sophia and Nathaniel Hawthorne were married in 1842, Mary and Horace Mann in 1843. In the 1850s both her parents died, the Hawthornes moved to England, and the Manns to Ohio.

With the financial demands of caring for ill parents, her concentration on adult education, publishing, and her bookshop, Elizabeth had less time to write. But in 1855 a group of her former students assembled a trust fund for her that gave her an income of $100 a year. This gave her some freedom from the daily pressures associated with earning a living and allowed her time to write. She did so prodigiously—on history, religion, philosophy, and a memoir.

When Horace Mann died in 1859, Mary moved to Concord, Massachusetts, and invited Elizabeth to move in with her and the children. Mary was working on publishing Mann's papers, and with her sister back in Massachusetts, Elizabeth once again turned her attention to early childhood education. She was convinced that free public education for the very young was the way to banish evil. Kindergartens in the slums would give a whole generation new hope for a better life and the moral conviction to achieve it. Elizabeth wrote and lectured prodigiously on education, but the turning point of her career came when she learned of the kindergarten movement founded in Germany by Friedrich Froebel. His methods involved planned programs of organized play, experiences with natural science, and physical activity. Children learned by doing, he professed, which appealed to Elizabeth's own hands-on style of teaching.

The following year, 1859, after intense study of Froebel's writings and correspondence with teachers in Germany, Elizabeth and Mary opened the first kindergarten in America. Although it was a private school, Elizabeth arranged for the school to be supported by donations, subsidizing those children whose families could not afford to pay. The kindergarten was a success, and the following year she moved it from Pickney Street to Winter Street, to a "quiet, high, sunny room with seven windows," as she described it in a letter to a friend. Many of her thirty students were children of her Boston friends. She was able to add to her teaching staff, hiring two assistants, a French teacher and a gymnastics instructor. The curriculum was well organized, following daily routines that included reading, arithmetic, singing, writing, and French. Gymnastics were central to the schedule, which although forming a set routine, was not in a classroom environment. Elizabeth saw this, as Froebel had, as a "garden where children were grown." The emphasis of the school was on creating an atmosphere where children would develop social skills and learn to make decisions based on a code of morality that would last a lifetime. The surroundings and routine were designed to stimulate and encourage children to grow and learn.

With a real and thriving school to demonstrate her theories in practice, Elizabeth's writings and opinions on early childhood education took on a new cachet. Educators and school officials struggling to set up fledgling public education systems sought her advice on setting up kindergartens. In 1863 Elizabeth and Mary published the *Moral Culture of Infancy and Kindergarten Guide*. Both theoretical and practical, the book included such details as lesson plans, setting up rooms, and what materials, games, and activities to use. She lectured and traveled to help establish kindergartens elsewhere, but never stopped studying to refine her theories and methods.

By 1867 Elizabeth had begun to worry that she had not fully understood Froebel's principle, and wanted to see in action those kindergartens that he had established. So from the proceeds of her writing and a series of adult history classes (supplemented by gifts from former students and a new wardrobe given her by an actress friend), she traveled to Germany and, at a grueling pace, visited kindergartens and met with leading educators.

Inspired by the singing children and their brightly colored toys and learning aids, Elizabeth returned to the States with new ideas and enthusiasm for her kindergarten crusade and immediately began to remake her own school to conform to what she had seen in Germany. She spoke to women's groups, recruited teachers, and worked to interest teachers' schools in adding kindergarten teaching to their curricula.

After revising her book and writing essays and articles for educational and scholarly journals, Elizabeth was invited to Washington, D.C., in 1871 to advise the Commissioner of Education on kindergartens. At last, almost entirely through her efforts, the Froebel concept of kindergartens was gaining recognition and popularity in education circles.

In 1873 Elizabeth founded the publication *Kindergarten Messenger*. The number of private kindergartens grew, and public ones began to be added to school systems. Free kindergartens were founded in poor neighborhoods and Pauline Agassiz Shaw, a wealthy woman who had been impressed with Elizabeth's work, donated her fortune to establish these throughout Boston. A few years later, Elizabeth merged the *Messenger* into the *New England Journal of Education*, feeling that by that time people understood the distinction between nursery schools, kindergartens, and primary schools, and with that hurdle jumped, kindergartens would get their fair share of attention from the scholarly journal.

Only then, in her eighties and losing her eyesight, did Elizabeth begin to slow down a bit. Her speaking appearances were fewer, but she was busy editing a book of her sister's. She had become a much loved and respected public figure, and if her dress was disheveled and her bonnet out of style, it just made her more endearingly eccentric in the eyes of her followers.

When she died, on January 3, 1894, a choir made up of kindergarten teachers sang the hymn "Lead Kindly Light." A settlement house for immigrants on Chambers Street in Cambridge was founded by friends in the kindergarten movement and dedicated to her memory. Peabody House opened with a free public kindergarten in 1896.

Elizabeth Peabody's unique contribution to the world was in her genius as a catalyst and conduit for ideas. She was able to grasp the importance of early education and the best methods for encouraging small children to learn, and she was able to translate those ideas into practice. Furthermore, she could communicate these ideas and methods to others. She was a gifted teacher, both of small children and of those who would teach them. And her energy, enthusiasm and determination created the momentum to make her dream of public kindergartens a reality.

• • •

Elizabeth Palmer Peabody is buried near her friends Ralph Waldo Emerson and Nathaniel Hawthorne in Sleepy Hollow Cemetery in Concord.

In 1978 Peabody House moved to a multicultural neighborhood on Broadway in Somerville, where it continues to provide childhood services, day care, and after school programs. A portrait of Elizabeth Peabody hangs on the wall.

The house at 13 West Street, near Boston Common, has a plaque next to the door, identifying it as the home of Peabody's influential bookshop and site of the meetings of the Transcendentalists. A bookstore again occupies the first floor.

LUCY LARCOM
(1824–1893)
SARAH BAGLEY
(1806–185?)

The Mill Girls: Fighting for Workers' Rights

*T*he Lowell mills, founded on the Merrimack River falls by Francis Cabot Lowell in 1822, turned a sleepy little village of five families into a company town of 18,000 within ten years. By 1845, thirty-three mills and more than 500 boarding houses supported a population of 30,000.

The mills—and the town—were run on a strict paternalistic system. Those who held power and made decisions lived in Boston, and the day-to-day management of each mill was carried out by an agent who had no power to make decisions. However altruistic the mills portrayed themselves to be, they had one purpose: to make a tidy profit for the Boston owners and investors.

The original Lowell mills had a clear hierarchy. At the top were the agents who lived in large houses, apart from the rest. Next were the supervisors of the workrooms and the highly skilled machinists, who lived in company housing. The third, and by far the largest, group was the "operatives"—as the mill girls were known—who lived in company-owned boarding houses. Below them were the laborers who dug canals and constructed buildings. These were men, mostly Irish, who lived in a shantytown called "The Acre."

Two of the most prolific chroniclers of the early mills were women who worked there in their youth and went on to become, respectively, a well-known writer and an active women's leader and suffragette.

Lucy Larcom moved to Lowell in 1835 with her widowed mother, who earned her family's living by running a company boarding house for mill girls. Lucy soon went to work in the mills, and was to work there for the next ten years. From an early age Lucy was precocious—an avid reader, writer, and poet. Later in life she would describe these years in a book, *A New England Girlhood*, and an article for *Atlantic Monthly*.

When Lucy's works first began to be published, she was writing poems and essays for *Lowell Offering* as well as other mill publications. In these first articles Lucy portrayed the owners of the mills as caring father-figures who were providing a wonderful opportunity for the women who worked there. She talked about the rules and discipline that the mill girls were subjected to, but wrote about it in a way that celebrated the structure and its benefits. Lucy was careful to let the reader know that the women did not complain about working conditions.

During this time Lucy also made it clear in her writings that the women did not support any strikes and would not be seen protesting. She stressed that they spent strike-time at home with their families, not causing a scene. Despite her overall positive tone, however, Lucy did hint at the disappointment some women felt after their high expectations regarding this opportunity to work met with reality.

When the mills were criticized by people seeking labor and social reform, Lucy rose to the mills' defense. To her, a criticism of

Portrait of Lucy Larcom by Augustus Marshall

the mill system and the working and living conditions there was a criticism of the women themselves, whose morality and virtue Lucy staunchly proclaimed. And she was largely right in this claim. With their little free time carefully regimented by the contracts they were forced to sign, there was hardly time or opportunity for female employees to be anything but virtuous. The activities of the mill girls, even outside the twelve to fourteen hours they spent at work, were closely watched. Pew rent for church was deducted from their pay and they were required to attend. (The male laborers, however, worked on Sunday.) The women could be fired for anything they did in their free time that the mill did not approve of. But to Lucy—and to many others—this paternalism was for the women's own good, and their work carried a nobility of its own, not without a touch of martyrdom. However, the mill girls and laborers could be fired for complaining or just for expressing an opinion contrary to an overseer's. This was most likely the biggest reason for Lucy's reluctance to write about the true working conditions inside the mills. The threat of losing her job was doubtlessly more of a motivator to keep quiet than her virtuous martyrdom.

Women came to the mills from all over New England for many reasons. Some came to earn money to support families at home and to send brothers to school. Others hoped to build a modest nest-egg for a dowry. A few hoped to earn money to fund an education for themselves. Some came to escape the tedium and even greater restrictions of farm life—for a taste of independence—since a woman's life in the early 1800s rarely included any chance to make decisions for herself. Until she was married and did what her husband chose, the typical woman's activities were closely directed by her father or brothers.

Lucy characterized the mills as the women's education, where they learned self-discipline, industry, and "incentive to labor."

Above all, these early mill girls—like Lucy—saw their time in the mills as brief and their goal was to rise out of it to a better life. Many saw passing through the mill system as a necessary stage in personal development.

It is interesting to note, however, that Lucy found a job in the mills that separated her from the working conditions suffered by most others. Lucy was a "drawer-in" who readied the looms for each new piece of fabric. This highly skilled job spared her the exposure to noise, dust-filled air, and hard labor that the rest of the women endured. Lucy's first job collecting spindles and a later one measuring fabric pieces in a finishing room were in far better surroundings and less stressful than her peers'. In all but the quieter finishing room, work hazards included machines thundering so loudly that in order to speak to someone one had to shout directly into another's ear; lint-filled air; heat from the machinery; and close quarters.

The reality of mill life for most of the women was quite grim. The women's lives were ruled by bells: wake up, go to the mill, begin and end half-hour lunches, go home, and at 10:00 P.M., curfew and lights out. Meal breaks were thirty minutes, during which time they had to leave the mills, run to their boarding houses to eat, then run back to work. If they were late in the morning or after meals, their pay was docked.

Workdays were from twelve to fourteen hours. Each woman had her own way of coping. Some trained their minds to shut out the noise. Fortunate women like Lucy, whose job gave her more freedom, leaned as far as possible out a window for fresh air and to escape the noise. The workday ended when it became too dark to operate the machines, and the women walked with companions slowly through the night to their boarding houses. But their conversation often turned to coughing from the lint-filled air they had breathed all day.

NATIONAL PARK SERVICE, COURTESY OF LOWELL NATIONAL HISTORICAL PARK

"Power Loom. One Girl Attends Four,"
from Eighty Years of Progress in the United States, *1867*

A tool for change was already forming, although the mill girls did not yet recognize it as such. A meeting in the attic of Lucy's mother's boarding house in 1837 had led to the forming of the Improvement Circle, a small group of women determined to use and improve their minds. This meeting was the first recorded literary club for women. More of these circles formed in Lowell, dedicated to self-improvement by reading the writings of their members and others at meetings. These meetings also served as a temporary distraction from work in the mills.

The group's first publications began as a means of getting their story out, of telling the public how they worked and what they did in their spare time. As a result of apprehensiveness over stirring up trouble with their bosses, the women only told half-truths about their experiences. The group also wanted to communicate with women in other mills. With the help of a local Universalist Church, they founded *Lowell Offering: A Repository of Original Articles, Written by Females Actively Employed in the Mills.* The first issue was distributed in October 1840. By the fifth issue it became a regular monthly magazine, very popular with mill girls and local residents.

At first the *Lowell Offering* was edited by the Universalist minister. After two years it was bought by a local newspaper and Harriot Curtis and Harriet Farley, both mill workers, became co-editors of the publication. The offering became the first magazine in America managed entirely by women. It was soon a respected example of an employee publication, praised by mill owners (it glorified the system and the owners) and other community leaders, and it began to garner both nationwide and overseas attention. The language was sentimental, according to the custom of the times, but its quality was equal to that of major women's magazines.

Because women didn't use their own names in print—thought immodest and unbecoming for females—most signed with initials or used pen names. The magazine published essays, short stories, poetry, and articles that proved the authors' literacy, intelligence, and concern for society. The magazine was published for five years, with more than fifty contributors, one of the best known being Lucy. Although over time the magazine changed its tone from sweet and romantic descriptions of life in the mills to essays that came closer to the truth as writers talked about their dreams for reform and respect in society, there were no cries for decent conditions, fair pay, or worker's rights. These types of sentiments were not allowed under the current editorship: "Those depend on circumstances over which we have no control," the female editors replied when challenged.

Lucy's descriptions of mill life were strongly in line with those of management. Sarah Bagley, a New Hampshire woman who had come to the mills in 1837 at age thirty-one, disagreed with Lucy's rosy portrayal of mill life. Rejecting the docile *Lowell Offering* that Lucy wrote for, Sarah founded her own paper, *The Voice of Industry*. She minced no words, sounding the call to fellow workers and condemning the mill owners and those who supported their myth of the happy working mill girls. The paper held the owners personally responsible, naming them and condemning them for the women's infested lodgings and unhealthy working conditions.

In December 1844, a group of fifteen women met to become an auxiliary to Lowell's Mechanics and Laborers Association. The group soon became more active than their parent organization, growing larger with each meeting. They formed the Lowell Female Labor Reform Association, with Sarah as president. Three months later, by the first convention of the New England Working Men's Association, they had 304 members. Sarah was elected corresponding secretary of the men's group, which was the first labor association to accept women as equals. Sarah spoke to the convention about the rights of women, reminding the men that women were counting on men to vote for measures to help *all* workers. In turn she pledged the women's full support for men's issues. By the end of the organization's first year, the Female Labor Reform Association had 600 members, with chapters in Waltham, Fall River, and at the New Hampshire mills. These organizations became social centers of their communities, at whose meetings both men and women worked together for their cause.

A skilled public speaker, Sarah taught classes for mill girls. She told her co-workers that they no longer had to do everything their employer or father told them. If they could earn money, they had a right to direct their own lives.

In 1845 Sarah was elected one of the vice presidents of the New England Workingmen's Association at its July 4 meeting. This was one of the few holidays mill workers had, so they chose it as their convention day. In her speech to the assembled workers, Sarah denounced the *Lowell Offering*, declaring that it was not the voice of the operatives, that it did not represent the truth, and that it was "controlled by the manufacturing interest to give a gloss to their inhumanity." Since in those days it was unbecoming for women to speak in public or to draw attention to themselves, Sarah and others in her cause were stigmatized—characterized in newspapers as "Amazons," "upstarts," and unbecoming to their sex, which discouraged many who otherwise may have joined the protests.

Sarah's attack on the *Lowell Offering* drew the indignation of its editors. Despite financial support by the mills (Sarah had been correct in this), the *Lowell Offering* ceased publication by the end of the year due to low sales. Sarah's *Voice of Industry* had become the voice of the working woman and man.

Sarah used the paper as a forum to ridicule the argument that girls were at the mills voluntarily, asking if anyone would actually work under such conditions if they had a reasonable choice. She pointed out that the alternative for these girls was abject poverty and that many of them had been sent to the mills to earn money to pay for their fathers' debts or brothers' education. They had not come of their own volition, she argued, and she likened their plight to slavery. She began working for a ten-hour workday, a right skilled workers had won elsewhere and that federal workers had won in 1840.

Thanks to Sarah and other activists, public attention was beginning to focus on conditions at the mills. It was clear to many that whatever early altruism there might have been in the mill system, it had given way to avarice. Housing had degenerated into filthy slums. Doctors spoke of the unsanitary working and living conditions and typhoid epidemics spreading in the crowded, unventilated workrooms. One physician complained to the American Medical Association that the conditions were far worse than those in prisons. Sarah took up this theme, visiting prisons and learning that prisoners condemned to hard labor worked four fewer hours a day than the mill women. Newspapers and social reformers began to investigate her claims.

The mills had their own supporters, however, including a Lowell minister who said if the women were sick, it was because they didn't take care of themselves and in their boredom ate too much candy. Mill owners said that if the women worked fewer hours, they would become immoral in their newfound free time.

Early strikes, beginning in the mid-1830s, showed that women workers could and would stand behind their convictions instead of backing down, and that they could organize themselves with dignity and composure. While not successful in the short run, these early strikes taught the women that they had some power in numbers. During an 1836 strike, citing principles of the American Revolution, the striking women formed the Factory Girls Association. They encouraged workers from the most important parts of the mill to join them. In two weeks they had all but 20 percent of the women on their side, and production ground to a near halt. Although nothing changed in terms of hours or pay, this time they were not fired and the women returned to their looms and spindles.

The mill girls' downfall in the early 1800s was their lack of negotiating skills: They could stop work, but in the end they could not bargain collectively. There was little history of workers of either sex negotiating with management, and women had the additional hurdle to overcome of being taught from birth not to argue with men.

Despite slow progress, the activists' message did spread. By the 1850s fewer women were looking at a prospective job at the mills as a step up. Soon, the combination of more successful strikes, the lack of vulnerable new female workers, and the onset of the Civil War and the resulting cotton shortages to northern mills slowed factory operations. Mills began to close rapidly, and those that didn't were more easily influenced by the political activities of their workers.

After inspiring one of the largest movements of her time, Sarah eventually left the mills to become the nation's first woman telegraph operator. Other women moved West to be teachers or join their pioneer families. Just as laborers had come a long way since the opening of the Lowell mills almost a century earlier, so had women, each generation building on the advances of their daring and articulate predecessors.

Although Lucy and Sarah had different methods, both were influential in the literature of their time. Lucy focused on enjoying her skill as a writer within the confines of the political pressure from her employers. She opened the door to writing about life in the Lowell mills. Sarah took the task a step further and brought it into the realm of activism, not only telling the whole truth about mill life but also venturing to criticize the owners and motivate other women to follow in her footsteps.

• • •

Lawrence Heritage State Park, in Lawrence, preserves old mill houses, where the stories of the workers and their struggles are shown in exhibits.

Lowell National Historic Park, at the Lowell mills, has a museum, a loom room with eighty-eight machines (now automated), and boarding houses to tour. Emphasis is on the later-arriving immigrant workers, showing their lives, the meager possessions brought from their homelands, and photographs.

The American Textile History Museum, near Lowell National Historic Park, also explores the textile mills and their products.

ELEANOR CREESY
1815–1900

Clipper Ship Navigator

Eleanor Creesy sat back in her chair and looked across the *Flying Cloud*'s small officers' cabin at her pacing husband. The captain made no effort to conceal his impatience.

"Don't just sit there and look at me," he exclaimed. "Tell me how far!"

Eleanor relished the moment for another instant, then looked down at the page of calculations on the table. She could scarcely believe the figures herself and had gone through the complicated math a second time just to be sure. "Three hundred seventy-four nautical miles."

She rose as she spoke, and he caught her up in his arms, kissing her in a burst of emotion rare even for married couples in the mid-1800s. "No ship has ever sailed that distance in twenty-four hours," he crowed. "The *Flying Cloud* is the fastest ship afloat." He held her at arms' length and added: "And you, my dear Ellen, are the finest navigator afloat."

When the *Flying Cloud* was piloted through the narrow channel of the Golden Gate, exactly a month later on August 31, 1851, the whole of San Francisco was abuzz. For the *Flying Cloud* had

Eleanor Creesy's clipper ship, the Flying Cloud

made the trip from New York in eighty-nine days and twenty-one hours, beating the previous record of ninety-six days and fifteen hours by a comfortable margin.

Captain Josiah Perkins Creesy Jr. and his navigator wife Eleanor were the toast of San Francisco, and as they danced and dined with the leading families, Eleanor couldn't help but think how close they had come to not arriving at all. The outcome of the trip had not always been certain—especially as the *Flying Cloud* floundered in storm-wracked seas, its broken mast ripping the rigging and tearing at the canvas sails as it swung wildly out of control in the wind.

Despite the record-breaking time, the voyage had been a long and difficult one. When Eleanor stood on the deck of the *Flying Cloud* as it sailed through New York's Verrazano Narrows into the Atlantic Ocean on June 2, 1851, she was well aware that the ship under her feet was setting to sea untested. It was the ship's shakedown cruise as well as its maiden voyage; its new design was untried. Its designer, Donald McKay, had given the *Flying Cloud* taller masts than any clipper at sea, and there was no way to predict accurately how they and all the canvas they carried would perform. As its navigator, Eleanor knew only too well what challenges lay ahead of her.

To further confound the passage, the *Flying Cloud* had set sail too late to catch the most favorable winds and currents for the dangerous passage around Cape Horn. Sailing southward in summer meant that Eleanor had to guide the *Flying Cloud* through the southern hemisphere seas in winter, when the west-bound ship would be sailing into the more forgiving prevailing winds as it rounded Cape Horn. And on entering the Pacific Ocean and turning northward, the *Flying Cloud* would have the least favorable season for making good time north of the equator.

To add to the uncertainty, Eleanor had determined to follow

not the tried and proven route used by other ships of the day as they sailed around South America, but a new route based on the scientific calculations and chartings of wind and current put forth in a new book by navigational expert Matthew Maury.

That her husband trusted her scientific knowledge and sea-going experience enough to agree to this daring experiment was a testament not only to Eleanor's skill but to Perkins's own confidence and character. Perkins was not a man who needed to show his own merit by belittling his wife's, and his recognition of her talents was the very basis of their marriage and their long partnership at sea.

The twenty-six-year-old Eleanor who had married this dashing captain in 1841 was not like the other delicate girls he knew in Marblehead. She was not afraid of the sea, even in its worst weather. In fact, Eleanor relished the feel of a deck heeling under her feet, and didn't mind at all that her face was tanned by sun and wind instead of staying fashionably porcelain-white under the protection of a parasol.

Eleanor's father, John Prentiss, was a schooner captain who saw no reason why his daughter (named after her mother Elinor) should not learn mathematics and navigation if they interested her. Plane and solid geometry would teach her logical thinking and sharpen her mind, he reasoned. Besides, in the twenty-four years between her birth in 1815 and that of her younger sister Abbie in 1839, Eleanor was John's only child. He gave her all the attention he would have given a son following in his footsteps.

Despite the disapproval of his Marblehead neighbors, John Prentiss made sure that Eleanor had a chance to practice and perfect her navigation skills on board his own ship. Eleanor shared her father's love of the sea, understanding the rhythms of the tides and currents and how they interplayed with the weather and the seasons and the stars. And these dependable rhythms attracted her far more than the unpredictable social tides that ruled life in little Marblehead.

Her mathematical education and her hands-on experience at sea were all but unheard of for a woman in mid-nineteenth-century Massachusetts. Young men, used to girls with a more traditionally "suitable" education, didn't quite know what to make of her intelligence. In turn, most hometown boys bored Eleanor—until she met one who had spent most of his time at sea since the age of fourteen. By the time Eleanor and Perkins were married, on June 3, 1841, she was at what was generally considered an unmarriageable age for a woman.

The very attributes that frightened off lesser men attracted Perkins to Eleanor. Here was a woman who could be his companion as an intellectual equal through the long months at sea. She was intelligent, understood the sea, and didn't quiver at the thought of a good storm. Her conversation was as fascinating as her ready smile was captivating. Her passion for sailing matched his own, and the fact that she was a skilled navigator was just the icing on their wedding cake.

By 1851, when Perkins took command of the *Flying Cloud*, the couple had traveled together for ten years, the last five aboard the tea clipper *Oneida*. Eleanor's home was the tiny captain's cabin she shared with Perkins. At thirty-six her face was already deeply lined from her years in the sun and wind, and her walk had more of the sailor's gait to it than the tiny steps of most women.

Eleanor's life was worlds away from that of the girls back home in Marblehead, with responsibilities and discomforts her girlhood friends never dreamed of. But it was a world of challenge that Eleanor thrived on. Navigating a sailing ship the size of the *Flying Cloud* required a delicate balancing act that weighed the set of the sail, the wind direction, ocean currents, the location of doldrums, the weather, and the skill of the ship's crew. It required

Eleanor's detailed knowledge of the location of the sun and stars, along with a thorough understanding of celestial navigation.

Speed in the clipper trade was half seamanship and half ship—its length, hull shape, and how much canvas it could carry. It took a strong and experienced captain to coax the most from the ship, just as it took a skilled navigator to guide it into the best combination of wind and currents. Perkins was a highly skilled captain, but a perfectionist and a man with fierce determination. It was not uncommon for him to disregard the opinions of his under officers when they wanted him to reduce the sail in bad weather. Perkins regarded a strong wind as an opportunity to make better speed, despite the increased dangers. But he was far from foolhardy or incautious, and he respected Eleanor's skills enough to listen to her opinions and accept her judgment. Little could Eleanor or John Prentiss have known that her unusual upbringing would prepare her so well for life with a man as liberal-minded as her father.

In addition to her duties as navigator, Eleanor was the ship's doctor and hostess to the passengers it carried. Curiously, although she navigated the most famous ship on the seas in a day when sailing ships were major news, no portrait of Eleanor exists. Not even an engraving of her accompanied the headline stories of the *Flying Cloud's* record-breaking voyages that led the news in cities around the world. We know from the letters of passengers that Eleanor was about five feet tall, wore her dark brown hair in a bun, and had warm hazel eyes, a delicate nose, and a ready smile. Their letters record that she was kind and sensitive to the feelings of those around her, that she was good-humored and sociable, and that she enjoyed poetry.

Day after day, much of her time at sea was spent setting the course, monitoring the wind and the ship's position, and comparing it to what she knew of each location's winds, currents, and shoals. Her responsibility was equal to that of the captain's in setting the course and the speed the great ship would travel. Her reliance upon more modern scientific methods, unlike those of other navigators of her day, meant that she needed to be meticulous in charting the ship's position.

Although Eleanor used the heavy sextant to determine their location astronomically, her navigation methods also involved understanding physical forces—what caused the winds to shift and change, and how these winds were affected by currents and seasonal variations. Eleanor had studied the works of controversial sea navigator Matthew Maury and understood his principles well. While Perkins would have the challenge of testing a new ship—the largest clipper on the seas—she looked forward to testing Maury's theories and the course his book provided.

In spite of the dangers of any sea voyage, and the added uncertainties of an untested ship and new navigation methods— or perhaps because of them—Eleanor sailed into the Atlantic on that June day full of excited anticipation. She had just spent more than a month visiting family and friends in Marblehead and readying the ship in New York, and both she and Perkins were ready to be at sea again. Although when not at sea they lived well in a luxury suite at the Astor House in New York, she was more at home in the tiny cabin of a clipper. And Eleanor preferred the company of the ship's officers and crew to the salons of New York and Boston. Not that the *Flying Cloud* was without its luxuries. A contemporary newspaper described its cabins as "most elegantly and tastefully wainscoted with satinwood, mahogany, and rosewood, set off by gilded pilasters."

Eleanor took a personal interest in the ship and its crew, and had seen to the provisioning of the ship herself. Sailors on the *Flying Cloud* were among the best fed seamen of their day, enjoying fresh meat twice a week. Along with the livestock—pigs, lambs, chickens, and turkeys—that provided this meat, Eleanor saw to it that the ship's stores were filled with barrels of salted pork, flour, molasses, smoked hams, dried beans and peas, salted fish, apples, onions, crackers, and tea. Blocks of ice were packed in sawdust to keep eggs, cheese, milk, cream, and vegetables fresh.

Eleanor had an added cause for excitement as she faced the Atlantic. The clipper *Surprise* had set a record of ninety-six days and fifteen hours on the westward voyage from New York to San Francisco, and the *Flying Cloud's* owner, Grinnell, Minturn & Co., offered Captain Perkins Creesy a handsome bonus if he could beat the record. In addition, the couple owned stock in the ship, so they would share further in the increased profits of a record-breaking trip. Speed was foremost in the minds of both captain and navigator as the winds caught the *Flying Cloud's* sails and carried them southward. At times the *Flying Cloud* seemed propelled on magic wings: The crew spent only three days in the dreaded doldrums north of the equator, where ships sometimes lay becalmed for weeks. At other times she seemed jinxed, as when the expected trade winds failed to blow, and the ship languished in the calm air.

Even before the dangerous passage around Cape Horn, the *Flying Cloud* and its crew were severely tested. As they sailed toward the equator, the crew began to notice a crack forming in the main mast, and everyone wondered if the timber would hold in heavy winds. Although the mast was 3 feet in diameter, it carried an enormous weight in canvas. In a storm, would the force of the wind, coupled with the increased weight of water on the sails and ropes, snap the mast and bring a tangle of twisting rope and canvas crashing down onto the deck?

There was no way to repair the mast at sea, so Perkins ordered the men to reinforce it with wooden splints and wrap it tightly in rope. His decision not to put in at Rio de Janeiro to have it repaired could have cost them the ship and the lives of everyone aboard, but the stop would have cost them valuable time in their race to beat the *Surprise*'s record.

Eleanor, too, had to make hard decisions in charting the winning combination of course and speed, based on her experiences and her knowledge of the sea and weather. And if she sometimes sailed closer to the edge of danger, it was because she was as excited as her husband by the race to beat the *Surprise*. The last thing she wanted was to hold the ship back by being overly cautious.

But the cracked and weakened mast was to haunt their voyage. On June 6, a clear day with high winds and seas, as Eleanor and Perkins sat down at midday to dine with their passengers as usual, dinner was disturbed by a loud crash from above, and the violent jerking of the ship. The captain jumped from his chair as passengers grabbed for the china and wine glasses sliding across the table.

On deck, Perkins saw what he feared most: the main topgallant pole mast hanging uselessly in a web of rigging almost 100 feet above his head. It was flying back and forth with each roll of the disabled ship, as though it were swinging in a giant hammock made of the tangled lines of the lower rigging that caught it as it fell. And with each wild swing its weight broke more lines.

As he assessed the damage and began to call out orders, the mizzen topgallant pole mast, weakened by the added pressure, also fell and hung about 60 feet above the poop deck. As each mast fell, it tore at the shrouds and stays, creating a continuous train of havoc overhead. At any moment the whole weight of masts, iron fittings, canvas, and rigging could fall, bringing with it the lower masts, spars, and rigging—tons of debris that could crush everyone and everything on the deck below.

Everything had to be untangled—masts, spars, sails and lines. The masts that were taken loose from the spars had to be lowered to the deck for repair, and it had to be done quickly before the swinging wood could beat the lower masts and rigging to bits. Men had to climb through the tangle and stand supported only by the yardarm footropes while they used both hands to untangle the snapping, twisting lines to free the masts. These they had to catch and secure before they could lower them safely to the deck. And all this had to be accomplished in tremendous wind, high in the air above a ship pitching disabled in a wind-lashed sea.

Times like this, when the skills of a navigator were not needed and all she could do was remain below and try to calm the fears of the passengers, were the most tedious of the whole voyage for Eleanor. She knew that she could be of no use above, but she understood the ship so well that she knew every danger that hung over her husband's—and her own—head. As Eleanor tried to make life bearable for passengers in the close quarters below, the men worked without rest until daylight failed. They continued all the next day and the following one, repairing the masts, mending the salvageable sail, and replacing the more than half that was beyond repair. On June 8 the *Flying Cloud* again caught the winds as a fully rigged ship, and Eleanor's life aboard returned to normal.

On August 29, only 600 miles out of San Francisco, another storm tore at the already weakened masts and rigging and this time it was the fore topgallant pole mast that broke loose, ripping the sails and crashing to the deck below before anyone could stop it. Only two days out of port, the crew repaired and hoisted the mast as they had the two before it.

Weather and broken masts were not the only challenges Eleanor and Perkins faced on the passage. The crew and officers of any clipper ship were a constant worry to its captain. It was hard to find able seamen who had the skill and bravery necessary to withstand the long hours and many hardships of life at sea. Although the best crewmen were loyal and professional in their work, some crewmen signed on just to get to the California gold fields, and others just needed to get out of town in a hurry. Some of these men were not happy about taking orders and doing the hard work required of the job, and were a threat to the safety of the ship. At one point during the *Flying Cloud's* voyage, a pair of disgruntled sailors drilled holes under their bunk and opened a hawsehole during a storm to allow sea water to run into the cargo hold. Fortunately their treachery was discovered before the precious cargo was ruined, but confining them behind iron bars left the ship short of badly needed hands.

Despite all the setbacks—the storms, a damaged mast, insubordination of their crew, and the less than optimal timing of the voyage—Eleanor and Perkins arrived in San Francisco in record time, making the *Flying Cloud* the most famous clipper ship of the Gold Rush era. It had been built purposely to make top speed on the dangerous Cape Horn route from New York to San Francisco, and proved well worth the owners' investment of $90,000—an unheard-of price for a ship in those days. After this trip the clipper's owners advertised space in its hold based on the *Flying Cloud's* record, proudly mentioning Captain Perkins Creesy in bold letters on the shipping broadsides. The navigator, of course, was not mentioned.

Getting goods from the East Coast to San Francisco was of major importance to people on both coasts. The Gold Rush was drawing men to California from all over the world, but the goods they needed fell far short of supply. Although San Francisco had a population of over 20,000, most people lived in tents and rough shacks built from salvaged ship timbers. Ships that had carried men west were often scuttled in the harbor because there were no passengers to pay for a return trip. Even the crews had jumped ship to try their luck in the goldfields.

Prices in San Francisco were astronomical—more than ten times the New York or Boston prices for barrels of pork or flour. Eastern merchants were so anxious to supply badly needed goods to the West that they would pay high shipping fees to clipper lines that could deliver merchandise faster than the long cross-continental wagon routes could get there. The *Flying Cloud* carried butter, flour, cheese, grain, soap, boots, dishes, cotton, candles, and clothing—all sold at top dollar in California.

As a team, Eleanor and Perkins continued to break records, besting the *Flying Cloud's* own maiden voyage time with a run of eighty-nine days and eight hours in 1854. That time was never beaten by a wooden clipper of the era. In fact, not until 1989, more than a century later, did a modern yacht record a better time—eighty days and nineteen hours. The *Flying Cloud's* voyage was much more than a sailboat race, however. The speed of the ship had a tremendous impact on the economic development of the West coast.

It is interesting to note that even modern maritime experts think it nearly impossible for a clipper ship to make the New York to San Francisco run in less than eighty-five days—and then only when everything is optimal. Even with perfect winds and weather, and no equipment breakdown or doldrums, it's unlikely. That the *Flying Cloud* made it in scarcely more than that as an untested ship, despite storms, broken masts, lost canvas, and an unfavorable sailing season, is a testament not only to its designer, the famous Donald McKay, but to the remarkable skills of both its captain and navigator.

Eleanor's role in the *Flying Cloud's* sterling performance was all the more unusual when we consider the role of women in the mid-nineteenth century. Not only were women not allowed to vote, they could not own property, or even keep the wages they earned. Women's education was geared to housekeeping tasks, and in the United States only one liberal arts college was open to women. While other captains occasionally took their wives along as companions on voyages, they were simply passengers, attending to the same wifely chores they would have overseen at home. But Eleanor worked side by side with Perkins throughout his career, navigating all the ships under his command.

The Creesys took the *Flying Cloud* on to Canton (Guangzhou) in southeast China from San Francisco, returning to New York in April 1852, where the couple was again treated to a hero's welcome. They continued on this profitable route around the world almost non-stop until 1855, when Perkins advised the owners that the *Flying Cloud* needed a thorough reconditioning.

At the peak of their career, the Creesys were paid $5,000 per voyage, while their counterparts were normally paid $3,000. In addition, they often earned an extra bonus for speed, so the couple was able to retire to a comfortable farmhouse near Marblehead. They timed their retirement well, since both the ship and the clipper trade had begun to decline. They left retirement only to bring the *Flying Cloud* back from San Francisco after her new captain had given up his command there. This last run was a particularly harrowing passage through the South China Sea, in 1855, when a storm drove the ship onto a coral reef and damaged it severely. Perkins directed the repairs of the ship at sea, while Eleanor stood watch with the spyglass, on the lookout for pirates or storms as the boat lay helpless. Upon safe return Perkins was feted in New York by the ship's owners, and upon accepting the set of silver they presented him in gratitude, he was quick to mention Eleanor's work and their partnership at sea.

Perkins came out of retirement once again to command another ship during the Civil War, returning to the farm in Marblehead in 1864. Eleanor, of course, did not accompany him on the military ship. Perkins died in 1871, and Eleanor survived him by nearly thirty years, dying in 1900.

Although the role of the *Flying Cloud* and the name of Captain Perkins Creesy is well known—they are included in nearly every history of sailing or description of the Golden Age of the clippers—Eleanor's role as navigator is almost never mentioned. Despite her lack of recognition, her role in the *Flying Cloud's* success was critical and her pioneering navigation around Cape Horn added significantly to the body of nineteenth century maritime knowledge.

• • •

The *Flying Cloud's* original logbook is at the Peabody Essex Museum in Salem, and letters of one of the passengers on that voyage are at the Marblehead Historical Society.

Eleanor and Perkins Creesy are buried in Harmony Grove Cemetery in Salem. Her headstone hints at nothing of her remarkable life at sea.

MARIA MITCHELL

1818–1889

Astronomer and Pioneer

*I*t was a chilly evening about half past ten, and Maria could hear the laughter and music from the party downstairs. But the sky was clear and inviting, and from her perch on the roof, she slowly moved her telescope to scan—bit by bit—a section of the night sky. Her eye moved over an unfamiliar light in the sky. Maria's face lit up as she centered the view and identified the bright spot as a comet. Flipping through her journals, she realized that this comet was not charted. She ran down the narrow stairs to her father's party and pulled him aside.

"Come up to the roof with me, father! I—I think I just discovered a comet!" Her father excused himself hastily and rushed upstairs with Maria. Confident in his daughter's abilities, he looked for a moment into the lens, then back at Maria.

"That's a comet; it certainly is!" he said, grinning from ear to ear. They spent the rest of the evening charting its course and gleefully wondering if they were the first to see this comet, both of them forgetting about the party below. "I'll send word to William Bond first thing in the morning!" Mr. Mitchell exclaimed.

Maria Mitchell

Maria Mitchell, born on August 1, 1818, was the third of ten children born to William and Lydia Mitchell of Nantucket, 30 miles off the Massachusetts coast. In addition to his position as headmaster at the local school and cashier at the Pacific Bank, William Mitchell was considered one of the best astronomers and surveyors on the island. In the early 1800s fishing and whaling were Nantucket's primary industries, and there was a great demand for someone who could survey the skies and set the various navigational devices used by sailors. As William conducted surveys for state and federal agencies, he found it helpful to have his curious young daughter Maria at his side to help record data and watch the skies with him. The two spent many nights in the widow's walk, a glass-enclosed cupola atop their Vestal Street home.

After Maria attended primary grades, she moved on to her father's school, which focused on the natural sciences. From there she spent a year in Cyrus Pierce's school and then became his assistant for a short time before opening her own school for girls when she was eighteen years old.

All through these years of formal education, it was what she learned at her father's side that was her true passion. When only twelve years old, Maria recorded and counted seconds while her father watched a solar eclipse—a job that had to be done with great precision. As Maria became more proficient with the tools of their trade, William would often leave her in charge of the surveys and calculations. The sky had to be observed every day of the year, and it was often Maria who sat with her eye to the scope. Their joint research and observations were so accurate and so consistent that the Mitchells were soon recognized on the mainland by both private institutions and federal agencies. Alexander Dallas, superintendent for the United States Coast Survey, chose their location to be an official survey station, with Maria and her father in charge.

The organization loaned William and Maria more advanced telescopes and equipment in return for supplying the data they needed. The official survey of the island lasted from 1835 to 1838, during which time Maria conducted many of the surveys, while still working at her other jobs. Her father was also appointed to the visiting committee of the Harvard College Observatory. Instead of being overshadowed by her father's titles, however, Maria benefited from his far-reaching connections in the scientific world, where he always gave her credit for her work. His scientific colleagues may have been surprised at his candor in sharing the credit with a young girl, but they grew to respect her work.

In 1836, while she was working with her father on the coastal survey, Maria was asked to be the librarian for the Nantucket Atheneum, a private library. She left her job as a teacher and became a student once more within the rows of books that surrounded her all day. Over the next twenty years that she held this title, Maria taught herself German, French, and advanced mathematics. Through her reading, she became familiar with some of the great writers and lecturers of the time, including Ralph Waldo Emerson and women's rights activist Lucy Stone.

Her interest in current events and social reform, encouraged by her friend Anna Gardner, was piqued when she attended the 1841 Nantucket Anti-Slavery Convention. Here she heard speakers that included women's rights activist Lucretia Mott, social reformer Wendell Philips, and abolitionists Frederick Douglass and Lydia Maria Child. Their ideas, and those she encountered in her reading, inspired her to think in terms of a world far larger than her island home.

After the publication of W. H. Smyth's 1844 book *Celestial Objects*, Maria and her father began to research and observe more complex phenomena of the sky, including double stars and variable stars. Along with watching Saturn and Venus, her two favorite planets, Maria became fascinated with the colors that she found within the stars themselves. She compared them to "a flower garden in autumn" and lamented to herself "What a pity that some of our manufacturers shouldn't be able to steal the secret of dyestuffs from the stars, and astonish the feminine taste by new brilliancy in fashion."

It was on the night of October 1, 1847, when Maria was twenty-nine years old, that she discovered the comet that had never been recorded before. Her father recorded the following in his observation notebook:

> 10 mo. 1, 1847—This evening at half past ten Maria discovered a telescopic comet five degrees above Polaris. Persuaded the [sic] no nebula could occupy that position unnoticed, it scarcely needed the evidence of motion to give it the character of a comet.

Her father immediately sent word of the discovery to his friends at the Harvard Observatory, as well as other astronomers. Many of them had larger, more powerful telescopes, but they confirmed that Maria had discovered this comet before them. Within two weeks it was confirmed that she had been the first to spot the comet in America, and on November 20, news came that she was the first in the world to discover it. The comet had been seen only two days later in Rome. It took almost a year for communications in the astronomical community to finalize it, but the discovery was finally named for her: "Miss Mitchell's Comet."

By this time, news of the remarkable discovery made by a woman had spread to Europe's scientific community. The King of Denmark, Frederic VI, sent Maria a gold medal to commemorate the achievement of being the first person to discover a telescopic comet. The award arrived on March 29, 1849, and bore the inscription *Non Frustra Signorum Obitus Speculamur et Ortus*, "Not in vain do we watch the setting and rising of the stars." Below the inscription was her name and the date of the discovery. This was not only the first time this prestigious European medal had been awarded to an American, it was the first time a woman had received the honor.

Recognition and fame for her discovery followed, and in 1848 Maria was honored as the first woman admitted into the American Academy of Arts and Sciences. She held this distinction until 1943, almost a century later. In the same year of her induction, an entire chapter of Elias Loomis's new book *The Recent Progress of Astronomy; Especially in the United States* was devoted to her work, entitled "Miss Mitchell's Comet." Maria wrote an account of her discovery and sent it to Joseph Henry, the director of the brand new Smithsonian Institution in Washington, D.C. He responded with a letter and a $100 reward—a substantial amount of money in the mid-nineteenth century—to mark her achievement.

Her career as a researcher and astronomer in her own right began to take off after the discovery of the comet. In 1849 she was hired to calculate the tables of Venus, one of her favorite subjects, by the American Nautical Almanac. Since she was being paid for the work, she became America's first professional female astronomer. In 1850 Maria was elected to the American Association for the Advancement of Science, and in 1853 she was awarded an honorary degree from Indiana Hanover College.

Although Maria's heart and soul were in astronomy and science, her new position in the world gave her the chance to travel and follow some of her interests as a citizen of a larger world than insular Nantucket. She relished each new adventure and treasured everything she learned from it. In 1857 Maria had the opportunity to tour the southern United States, journeying with friends on the *Magnolia* down the Mississippi River. When the *Magnolia* became stuck in a sandbar, the party moved to a smaller boat, the *Woodruff,* and continued exploring the South. Here Maria saw firsthand some of the conditions she had read about and heard described at antislavery meetings at home. The experience began to truly broaden her limited island experiences.

In June of that same year, only a month after returning from the South, Maria left home again, this time for Europe. She sailed on the *Arabia*, which left New York on June 22, arriving in England eleven days later. In England Maria visited several prominent astronomers, including John Hartnup and John Taylor at the Liverpool Observatory, and William Lassell at his home observatory. George Bond, astronomer and son of the Harvard College Observatory director William Cranch Bond, had given Maria a letter of introduction when she left for Europe, stating that "this lady whose scientific attainments have placed her among our first American astronomers . . . adds an extensive acquaintance with mathematics and astronomy, and is herself an accomplished and experienced observer." In many places, however, Maria was surprised to find that this introduction was unnecessary: Her name and accomplishments had been known for years among British scientists.

Maria settled for a while in London, finding a place with a nice view of Burlington Gardens. While living there, she wrote in her journal: "There are four great men whose haunts I mean to seek out, and on whose footprints I mean to stand—Newton, Shakespeare, Milton, and Johnson." She visited Westminster Abbey to find their graves, and sought out the places associated with their work: where Samuel Johnson wrote, and Sir Isaac Newton's observatory. It is interesting—and indicative of Maria's increasing breadth of interest—that only one of these four great heroes she sought was a scientist.

After enjoying the beauty of the English countryside and meeting English astronomers, Maria moved on to Paris. Here she enjoyed a different sort of touring. She loved to walk through the Paris markets, watching people and absorbing French culture in the raw. She visited the Louvre and the library of the Conservatoire, and was overwhelmed by the masses of great works at her fingertips. The Catholic churches, with their grandeur and rich ornamentation, attracted her. But when Maria went to the observatory, she was met with surprising resistance by its director, Jean Joseph Leverrier. This reception was quite a contrast to the warm welcome she had received from English colleagues. Before long, she moved on to Rome.

There Maria stayed with fellow Massachusetts natives Nathaniel Hawthorne and his wife, Sophia. The Hawthornes adored Maria and it was not long before their children were calling her "Aunt Maria." The Hawthornes' son Julian later wrote about her with great fondness, giving us a rare insight into Maria's personality:

> There was a charming quaintness and innocence about her and an immense healthy curiosity about this new old world and its contents. She had a great flow of native, spontaneous humor, and could not say anything that was not juicy and poignant. She was old fashioned, yet full of modern impulses and tendencies; warm hearted and impulsive, but rich in a homely common sense.

In Rome she visited the famous sites, going several times to Saint Peter's Basilica. Maria loved Rome and spent a good deal of time engaged in her favorite pastime of observing people. She thoroughly enjoyed the Hawthorne family, although she never felt as though she had the opportunity to truly know Nathaniel. She was there when he started writing *The Marble Faun*, and later when it was released and she read the work, she was delighted to see a bit about herself in its pages: "The woman's eye that has discovered a new star turns from its glory to send the polished little instrument gleaming along the hem of her kerchief or to darn a casual fray in her dress."

Much as Maria loved Rome and the company of the Hawthornes, she was curious to see more places. Her next stop was Florence, where she met one of her inspirations, the independent-minded mathematician Mary Somerville. Describing her new friend and her exceptional talent and passion for her work, Maria distinguished between the mathematical scholar and the mathematician—a distinction that could equally well apply to her own relationship with astronomy:

> Some memorize and become very learned . . . like any other result of mere memory. . . . The true mathematician joins his mathematics to all science. Of what interest is the discovery of a new curve if no flower winds itself according to its laws, if no bird builds to interpret its sinuous ways, if no planet or star follows its sweeping arches.

In Mary Somerville, Maria had found a kindred spirit, a scholar who sought to fit her scientific passions into the wholeness of life.

Then it was on to Germany. After a hearty welcome by naturalist Alexander von Humboldt in Berlin, Maria traveled back to England. Having already pursued her scientific interests there, she chose to close her European adventures by hearing one of the writers whose works she had read while working at the Nantucket Atheneum, Charles Dickens. After attending a reading by Dickens, she confided to her journal: "He had a foppish look—is small, dark-haired; he wore a bunch of flowers on the left side buttonhole of his coat. . . . Mr. Dickens shows a good deal of the actor —especially in the mirthful touches."

Maria arrived back in the States in 1858 to a very sick mother. Lydia Mitchell no longer remembered her daughter, and lived in this state for three more years until her death. This was one of the most difficult periods in Maria's life. Not only was she watching life drain out of her mother, but the confinement it brought came right after some of Maria's freest and most stimulating and invigorating months.

One bright point during this time was a gift from the "Women of America." The spokeswoman, Elizabeth Peabody, sent Maria a new 5-inch telescope. It was far larger and nicer than any she had owned before and became Maria's most prized possession. Helped by the improved quality of her tools, Maria continued to discover and calculate, and wrote for many journals about double stars, sunspots, meteors, and eclipses.

After her mother died in 1861, Maria decided to move to Lynn with her father to be closer to her sister Kate. Although the observatory came with them, Maria felt unchallenged and missed the Nantucket Atheneum, where she had spent so much time.

Maria's life was soon to change, however. She received a letter from Rufus Babcock on behalf of Matthew Vassar, dated August 21, 1862. In it Babcock asked Maria to come to New York to interview for a faculty position. But soon Babcock himself arrived in Lynn to persuade Maria to become a professor at Mr. Vassar's new women's college in Poughkeepsie, New York. The academic world's confidence in her was clear in a letter of recommendation from Alphonsus Crosby of the Salem Normal School:

> I should consider the Trustees of the Vassar Female
> College eminently fortunate if they could secure
> the services of Miss Maria Mitchell as Professor of
> Astronomy. Her distinguished scientific attain-
> ments, her liberal literary culture, the remarkable

successes and honors which she has already attained, her signal industry and zeal in the promotion of science, her fondness and ease of character, unite in commending her as preeminently fitted for this position in an institution so nobly endowed.

Other similar letters of recommendation came from astronomy and mathematics professor Benjamin Pierce of Harvard College and Alexis Caswell, the president of Brown University. Although Maria responded at first with only moderate interest, in the end she accepted the position. After a few years of waiting for the completion of the college, Maria joined the rest of the new faculty at Vassar Female College in 1865 as professor and director of the observatory. Here she had use of the country's third-largest telescope—at 12 inches, more than twice the size of her own prized piece of equipment.

The first few years of the college brought some controversy as to whether female students could hold up under the pressure of rigorous college courses. On this debate, Maria had several characteristically pointed comments to add, including: "It is better to spend an hour watching the habits of an ant than trying to put up the hair fantastically." She also commented that "Nature made woman an observer. . . . So many of the natural sciences are well fitted for woman's power of minute observation that it seems strange that the hammer of the geologist is not seen in her hand or the tin box of the botanist."

Maria had a special relationship with her students, whom she considered partners—instead of merely pupils—in learning. This attitude was exemplified in her message to the class of 1876, when she told them, "We are women studying together." Her classes took field trips with her to see eclipses, and she encouraged a range of interests in the natural sciences. Students described her class-room as unique, with an atmosphere different from any other class. An astonishing testament to her skills not only as a teacher but as a woman who encouraged greatness by her own example is the fact that twenty-five of her students went on to be featured in *Who's Who in America*. She inspired and instructed well-known scientists, including physicist and astronomer Christine Ladd-Franklin and chemist Ellen Swallow Richards, and taught her own successor, Mary W. Whitney. In 1869 Maria was honored as the first woman elected to the American Philosophical Society.

Since her move from a private observatory, Maria had become more aware of the discrimination against women in the sciences. Even at Vassar, the trustees had doubted the abilities of female fac-ulty. Because of her own personal experience, Maria was moved to found the Association for the Advancement of Women in 1873. In one of her letters from the early days of this organization, she wrote:

> Women, more than men, are bound by tradition and authority. What the father, the brother, the doctor and the minister have said has been received undoubtingly. Until women throw off their rever-ence for authority, they will not develop. When they do this, when they come to truth through their investigations, when doubts lead them to dis-covery, the truth which they get will be theirs and their minds will go on and on unfettered.

Her influence at Vassar continued for more than twenty years, dur-ing which time she was elected vice-president of the American Social Science Association. She retired in 1888, and moved back to Lynn. The next year, in 1889, Maria died at seventy years old. She is buried on Nantucket.

So deep was Maria's impact on her former students from Vassar that they began to visit Nantucket to see her grave and find the observatory where her first discoveries were made. Because of this interest and their own love for her, a group of relatives and friends founded the Maria Mitchell Association in 1902. First the organization bought her childhood Vestal Street home, and later built an observatory on the outskirts of town. In 1920 the association acquired her father's old schoolhouse, making it into a library dedicated to books on astronomy and the natural sciences. On September 24, 1994, more than a century after her death, Maria Mitchell was inducted into the National Women's Hall of Fame.

• • •

The Nantucket-based Maria Mitchell Association is still thriving, now a center for learning in all the natural sciences—a fitting tribute to Maria's own quest for truth. The Historic Mitchell House, a science library, and an observatory are on Vestal Street, and the Loines Observatory, also operated by the association, is located at 59 Milk Street. The association also oversees the Hinchman House Natural Science Museum, on Vestal Street, and an aquarium on Washington Street. Maria is buried near her original home.

JULIA WARD HOWE
1819–1910

"Mine Eyes Have Seen the Glory"

Early in the morning, Julia rose and found her pen and paper. The words had finally come to her, and she had to write them down before she forgot them. In the dim light Julia scribbled the lines that rang through her head until she was satisfied that she had committed them to memory.

> *Mine eyes have seen the glory of the coming of the Lord*
> *He is trampling out the vintage where the grapes of wrath are stored*
> *He has loosed the fateful lightening of His terrible swift sword*
> *His truth is marching on . . .*

Julia lay back down in her bed and closed her eyes, feeling excited about her verses. She knew at that moment that something very important had just occurred.

This was the birth of the "Battle Hymn of the Republic," as described by Julia Ward Howe in later years. Encouraged by friend and Unitarian minister James Freeman Clarke, Julia had set the words of her new patriotic poem to the Civil War tune "John Brown's Body." That "something of importance" that Julia felt was her emergence as a recognized poet, well known to this day.

Julia Ward was born to Samuel Ward and Julia Rush Cutler Ward on May 27, 1819. Named for a sister who had died at four years old, Julia was one of six surviving children. She loved her mother dearly, considering her "the first and dearest of friends." Although only five years old at the time of her mother's death, Julia always remembered that last summer with her mother, who died giving birth to another daughter, Annie. Julia recalls waking up that day to her father's words: "Julia, your mother is dead." The family suffered great sorrow and her father became very ill, during which time Samuel would have nothing to do with baby Annie. It was not until Julia's grandfather came to visit and learned of Samuel's emotional breakdown, forcing Samuel to hold his youngest, that the child was welcomed into the family.

Samuel took it upon himself thereafter to be both mother and father to his children, and he began to run a strict household in reverence to his late wife's strong religious views. He asked the children's aunt to help around the house, but paid close attention to the upbringing of his children. Education was very important in Samuel's eyes, and he provided the best tutors for his children. Although he forbade attendance at the opera or plays, he made sure that his girls were well trained in music and voice lessons. The education of his daughters was not limited to traditionally feminine pursuits, however. Julia and her siblings studied philosophy, algebra, geometry, chemistry, and foreign languages. At fourteen years old, Julia asked her father to hire an Italian tutor, Italian being her third spoken language. She was a child of high spirit and aspirations. Even at a young age, Julia had the sense that she would be an influential writer, contributing a great work to the world.

In her late teens Julia suffered two great losses that changed her focus from that of scholarly devotion to religious devotion. Both Julia's brother and father died within a short time of each

Julia Ward Howe

other, in 1839, and she began to read the Bible almost constantly for nearly two years until a friend lent her *Guizot's History of Civilization*. It was this book that opened her eyes to a life of action and purpose, beyond the contemplative state of religious studies. Her views on life and religion began to change, and she began to participate in life again.

Julia met her future husband, Samuel Gridley Howe, when she was twenty-two, soon after her revelation. She was impressed by his work as a doctor—the first to teach a blind deaf-mute how to utilize language—as well as his dedication to being a spokesman for the disadvantaged many and their innate rights as humans. Engaged in late 1842, the couple was married on April 23, 1843, and immediately left for a year-and-a-half honeymoon trip to Europe. During this time their first child was born. Upon returning home they took up residence at the Institute for the Blind in South Boston, where Dr. Howe became the director. A couple of miles from the city and in an undesirable section of town, Julia began to feel quite isolated from her friends and her usual way of life. Befriending the teachers at the school gave her the opportunity to reach out somewhat, but the constant stream of entertaining caused her more anxiety than relief. Julia was far from at ease with hosting dinner parties for her husband's esteemed acquaintances, and would rather have spent time on reading and studying, while her sister picked up the domestic slack. She describes the reason for her lack of success with household upkeep this way: "I was by nature far from observant, and often passed through a room without much notion of its condition or contents, my thoughts being intent on other matters." In her autobiography, *Reminiscences*, Julia recalls the follies of her first few attempts at housewifery, including a determination to learn how to cook from one of the prominent books of the time. After tasting her "experiments," Dr. Howe hired a housekeeper and lifted a huge burden from his wife's domestic stresses.

Her family's close affiliation with the prominent intellectuals of Boston was not lost on Julia, however. Attending dinner parties and banquets with her well-respected husband gave her the chance to meet the greatest thinkers and activists of her time, including Margaret Fuller, Ralph Waldo Emerson, and Horace Mann. It was through these acquaintances that Julia was exposed to the transcendentalist movement that was sweeping a breath of fresh air over a Puritan society. She began to attend the lectures of Theodore Parker, a prominent preacher of transcendental thought. Although society friends disapproved, Julia continued to attend and discuss this new way of looking at her world with like-thinkers, and soon felt a great relief from the tyrannical bonds imposed by the strict religion of her parents. She became affiliated with the Unitarian church, finding a home amongst those who saw God as a loving and understanding figure instead of a wrathful tyrant.

Over the years five more children were born to Julia and Samuel. Yet Julia still made a place for her studies. She read voraciously, not only in English but also in French, Italian, German, Greek, and Latin. She was impressed by the liberal thinking of Cicero, and speculated that people of his time were more forward-thinking than her contemporaries in respect to ethics. Later in life she would identify herself as a lifelong student, although she was always the first to point out that she had no formal education beyond the tutelage of her youth. "I have only drawn from history and philosophy some understanding of human life, some lessons in the value of thought for thought's sake, and, above all, a sense of the dignity of character above every other dignity. . . . I have followed the great masters with my heart."

Although her husband was often discouraging and negative about her intellectual pursuits, as well as unhappy about her inability to keep an orderly house, this did not prevent Julia from becoming active in the causes she felt worthy. She joined the discussions of the Boston Radical Club, with Dr. Howe, where she met and heard great authors and orators like Oliver Wendell Holmes, John Weiss, and Charles Dickens. Much to her husband's unhappiness, she herself began to speak at these meetings and share her thoughts on ethics and philosophy. Despite this show of confidence, Julia still chose to publish her first collection of poetry, *Passion Flowers* (1854), under a pseudonym for fear of her husband's disapproval.

Julia's poems had been published since she was fourteen years old, yet her big break came with the patriotic and inspiring "Battle Hymn of the Republic" in 1861, presented and published under her real name. It took Boston by storm, and Julia was finally regarded as an individual instead of just "Dr. Howe's wife." Her previous works had garnered only marginal attention by reviewers and the public. *Passion Flowers* was soon followed by *Words for the Hour,* which was described by Lucia Gilbert Calhoun in an early biography as "wayward, inartistic, obscure, defiant, but . . . riper, and even more full of promise (than *Passion Flowers*)." Julia also wrote editorials and articles for her husband's antislavery paper, *The Commonwealth;* a play that was produced but did not take off; and accounts of 1859 travels to Cuba with Dr. Howe. A testament to her success and fame is her biography's inclusion in the 1869 *Eminent Women of the Age: Being Narratives of the Lives and Deeds of the Most Prominent Women of the Present Generation.* Lucia Gilbert Calhoun gives her impression of Julia:

> She has auburn hair, and large, sad eyes, "where soul seems concentrate in sight." Her mouth is her fine and expressive feature, though her whole face is mobile. Her bell-like voice and her pure enunciation have a charm like music, and the eloquence of her fine hands is irresistible; her wit is brilliant,

ready, merciless, and her sarcasm polished and swift as the axe of the headsman Rudolph. Her friends know that music is her passion, swaying her whole being; that the drama is to her the Beautiful Art . . . that she found the infancy of her children a constant miracle of beauty, and that now, they pet and rule her as if she were the child; that the dignity of her nature, forcing her to accept simplicity as the best good, makes all luxurious and showy living as the best to her, while her sense of symmetry and harmony delights in order and elegance.

In early 1872 Julia convinced her husband to send her to London, where she attended the Woman's Peace Congress. Inspired by this convention and its attendants, she launched a month-long lecture series on Sundays at the Freemason's Tavern, where the room was readily filled with eager attendants. After Julia was asked to speak for the Unitarian Association, she hoped to have her moment in front of the English Peace Society, but was rejected because women weren't allowed to speak there. She referred to her mission as "my plea for a combination of women in behalf of a world's peace." Her travels during this time allowed her to meet many more prominent thinkers and writers and had an impact on her belief system concerning women in the political arena.

Because of her trip to London, Julia was inspired to begin a yearly tradition to gather and discuss "the advocacy of peace doctrines." For this she chose the name "Mother's Day" and the date June 2, reasoning that it was a "time when flowers are abundant, and when weather usually allows of open-air meetings." Her movement was successful, and although no longer celebrated as a day of meditation on peace, the holiday is obviously alive and well today.

The 1876 death of Dr. Howe had a significant effect on Julia's career as an activist and views on women. The woman who once described marriage as being "like death . . . a debt we owe to nature," was suddenly free to travel as she wished and speak freely without fear of ridicule from her husband. She also had the opportunity to spend more time with other women and cultivate stronger friendships with them. She gained a new respect for women now that she was freed from her husband's negating attitude and the constant self-comparison she had always made with him. Identifying herself once as a "wife over-shadowed for [a] time by the splendor of her husband's reputation," she began to regard her accomplishments in their own right, not as they fell in comparison with his, and in kind began to see other women in the same refreshed light. She describes her metamorphosis:

> During the first two thirds of my life I looked to the masculine ideal of character as the only true one. . . . The new domain now made clear to me was that of true womanhood,—woman no longer in her ancillary relation to her opposite, man, but in her direct relation to the divine plan and purpose, as a free agent, fully sharing with man every human right and every human responsibility. This discovery was like the addition of a new continent to the map of the world, or of a new testament to the old ordinances.

In addition to this profound change in the way she looked at women, Julia was questioning a woman's place in society. With the end of the Civil War came the emancipation and full citizenship rights for slaves. Although her wording was somewhat racist and elitist, Julia wrote and spoke about the glaring inconsistencies of current civil rights. She also, as many other women did, felt bitter about all of the effort she had put into the freedom of slaves, only to find herself and other women denied certain freedoms. She recalls the sting of rejection, "The women of the North had greatly helped to open the door which admitted him [African-Americans] to freedom and its safeguard, the ballot. Was this door to be shut in their [women's] face?"

It is after these transformations of character and opinion, during the late 1870s, that Julia began to work with the suffrage movement. Joining a group which would soon call itself the New England Women's Club, she began her campaign for equal rights with a determination to keep it in a "very liberal and friendly spirit, without bitterness or extravagance." As an outsider of the suffrage movement for so long, Julia was aware of the image society had of the suffragettes, that of bitter and aged spinsters. Julia wanted to change that falsity and convince even the most dubious to at least consider the activists' plea. She even acknowledged her own prejudice before she had met the leaders of the cause, describing the first time she met the outspoken early feminist Lucy Stone, "who had long been the object of one of my imaginary dislikes. As I looked into her sweet, womanly face and heard her earnest voice, I felt that the object of my distaste had been a mere phantom, conjured up by silly and senseless misrepresentations."

With these newfound friends, Julia finally began to feel like she belonged. She was with people who held common ideals and was free to be as dedicated to the cause as she wanted. Plunging headfirst into service, she immediately made Lucy Stone a mentor. Lucy taught Julia how to speak more effectively and to larger groups. They often worked together on presentations that they brought to eastern and midwestern cities as far as Denver, as well as small towns across the East. They found resistance wherever they went, but listeners gathered even in the smallest of towns. In some places they were met with strong resistance, only to have the protestors quiet and listen to their speeches, eventually cheering them on.

As the group's reputation grew and the cause became a public concern, Julia was invited to attend legislative hearings and speak at these events. She recalled one hearing during which a woman remonstrated the women's suffrage movement, and ended her speech with her opinion: "No woman should be allowed the right of suffrage until every woman shall be perfectly wise, perfectly pure, and perfectly good." Although not permitted to respond at the time, Julia later challenged, "If, as is just, we should apply the test proposed by (this woman) to the men of the community, how long would it be before they could properly claim the privilege of the franchise?"

Over the years Julia was a member of over twenty clubs and societies, many of which she founded and chaired. Julia was the president of the New England Women's Club from 1871 until her death in 1910. Among her other clubs and associations were American Woman Suffrage Association (AWSA), the Saturday Morning Club for teenage women, the International Women's Peace Association, and the Association for the Advancement of Women. Julia believed that clubs were vital to a woman's self-esteem and that an active social life that engaged in worthy causes was the duty of an educated woman.

Her campaign for suffrage focused on a few essential points that Julia stressed regularly in her many speeches. One of her most heartfelt claims was that a woman's right to vote would bring the family closer together, because husbands and wives would be on more equal footing. She also felt that a woman's right to vote would raise "the average of political honesty among the voters" and make "elections and political meetings more orderly." She also described the impact this would have on all women, helping their self-esteem and expanding their intellectual world. Julia was also convinced that women were essential to the proper reform of laws and that her sex would bring much needed wisdom and variety to the election process.

In 1899 Julia published her autobiography, *Reminiscences*. This book gives us a front-row seat to many of her opinions, yet only lightly touches on her life with her husband, as she stays focused on her crusade. In 1908 Julia was honored as the first woman to be elected to the American Academy of Arts and Letters.

She died on October 17, 1910.

Julia used her maternal image and society influence to benefit the suffrage movement. She was a sympathetic spokesperson, who often pulled in imagery from the Bible and patriotic scenes to bring her audience to her point of view. After almost forty years of passionate service for the suffrage movement, Julia became an expert orator and debater.

• • •

In 1988, the U.S. Postal Service issued a stamp honoring Julia Ward Howe, author of "The Battle Hymn of the Republic."

Besides songwriting, Howe is best known for promoting Mother's Day. Horrified by the carnage of the Civil War, Howe began organizing and paying for an annual Mother's Day for Peace gathering in Boston, for at least ten years, beginning in 1873. Over time, the peace aspect of Mother's Day faded into history.

ELLEN SWALLOW RICHARDS

1842–1911

Champion of the Scientific Home

*O*f course, Miss Swallow, you do understand that it would be impossible for an institution of the stature of the Massachusetts Institute of Technology to award you a degree."

"I realize that," replied the serious young woman, with an agreeable smile. "I will be satisfied just to be able to join the male students in the classroom in order to learn. And," she continued pleasantly, "a few women's skills may to be useful to you and other members of your faculty. After all, laboratories need cleaning just like kitchens do."

Three years later, in 1874, MIT awarded Ellen the bachelor of chemistry degree she had earned alongside male students. Her work would take her far beyond anything either she or that dean dreamed of that morning in his Boylston Street office in Boston— and far beyond that of many of her male classmates, as well.

It would be fourteen years before women would be admitted to MIT as full students, and the school never awarded Ellen the doctorate degree she earned there. But she received the education she sought, and paved the way for generations of women who would follow her.

Ellen Swallow Richards

Ellen Swallow was born in Dunstable, Massachusetts, on December 3, 1842, the only child of Fanny and Peter Swallow. Both parents were schoolteachers, and they operated a farm as well. Ellen helped on the farm and was taught at home, where she learned housekeeping skills along with Latin, French, and mathematics. Her needlework and cooking skills won her prizes at the county fair, even though she was considered a bit of a tomboy.

When she was seventeen, her family moved to Westford, where her father opened a store. Here Ellen was fortunate enough to begin attending formal school at Westford Academy. Four years later the family moved again, this time to Littleton, where she again worked in her father's store. Ellen continued her voracious reading and studying in her spare time.

She also taught school in Littleton, but her mother's increasingly ill health made the extra work difficult. Ellen's own health began to show the strain of being responsible for duties at home, her father's store, and in the classroom, all while trying to follow her own pursuits. Although she had hoped to save enough money for college, she soon had to abandon her teaching career in order to help out at home. She later described her depression during this period as "two years in Purgatory."

By 1868, when she was twenty-five, Ellen was finally able to attend Vassar College, where she was a very serious student. Older than her classmates, she tended to her studies instead of a social life. Her excellent work brought her income as a tutor in Latin and mathematics, and she was able to pay her tuition from these earnings and from money she borrowed.

Thriving in this academic atmosphere, her good health returned, in turn ending the depression she had suffered the previous few years. The two years Ellen spent at Vassar introduced her to the world of science, and she developed special interests in chemistry and astronomy. She studied the latter under professor

Maria Mitchell and for a time after her graduation she considered becoming an astronomy teacher. Chemistry ultimately won out, perhaps because in it Ellen saw her chance to change the world. She mentioned in letters to her parents during her senior year at Vassar how exciting it was to learn about the great opportunities for solving everyday problems through science. Ellen felt that her increased expertise in chemistry would be useful to her father's new business of manufacturing building stone.

When Ellen gathered all the self-confidence she could muster and applied to the Massachusetts Institute of Technology, the school had only been in existence for five years. Already it was seen as the finest school for advanced learning in the sciences, using innovative techniques of teaching through experience in laboratories instead of only in the classroom. She was gratified that the school accepted her, even though it was as a "special student," and did not charge her the usual tuition.

What Ellen didn't know was that the president of MIT rationalized that if she were not paying tuition, he could say that Ellen was not considered a true student. If a trustee or male student complained of a woman in the classroom, the president could truthfully say that she was just sitting in on classes but was not registered as a student. Years later, when Ellen discovered that this was the reason she was not charged full tuition, she said that she would not have accepted admittance to the school under those terms.

Ellen was not, however, a feminist of the usual stripe. It was she who suggested that her "womanly skills" might be useful to her male professors: She mended their clothing, cleaned the laboratories, and otherwise made herself useful in a traditional female role in order to retain her place in the classroom and laboratory. This willingness to accept the usual women's position and responsibilities, while studying and working in a "man's" profession, would continue to characterize her attitude toward issues such as women's suffrage and equality throughout her career. Her letters while at MIT reflect the careful path she trod. She was quite conscious that everything she did paved the way for other women to follow. "Perhaps the fact that I am not a radical or a believer in the all-powerful ballot for women to right her wrongs and that I do not scorn womanly duties . . . is winning me stronger allies than anything else," she wrote. Ellen's neat appearance, well-organized mind, and seemingly inexhaustible energy also impressed those who knew her.

In 1873 MIT did award Ellen the bachelor's degree she had earned, and in that same year Vassar granted her a master's degree based on her concurrent work there and a thesis on the composition of iron ore deposits. She continued her graduate studies at MIT for two more years, but was refused a doctorate degree. Her husband—a member of the MIT faculty—writing about this incident later, related that Ellen was refused the degree because MIT had not previously awarded a doctorate in chemistry. The department heads did not, he said, want the first such degree granted to a woman.

Ellen had met Professor Robert Hallowell Richards while still a student at MIT. This handsome young scientist was responsible for creating MIT's mining and metallurgical program and laboratories, which remain one of MIT's outstanding fields to this day. Fitting to their mutual scientific passions, he proposed marriage to Ellen in the chemistry lab. Ellen had just been awarded her bachelor's degree from MIT. The couple was married on June 4, 1875, when she was thirty-three. Their marriage would make it possible for Ellen to follow her career with more ease, both because of financial security and because her husband considered her an equal partner. This cachet made it more difficult for male scientists to look patronizingly on her or on her work.

The first several summers of their marriage were spent traveling with Robert's mining students. Ellen was the team's chemist, as well as its unofficial "house mother," a role she enjoyed even when she and her husband were at home during the school year. In 1881 and 1882 the Richards spent their summers in northern Michigan, where Robert was engaged in copper ore research. Ellen's advanced knowledge of chemistry was useful to Robert's work with metals, and she helped him keep abreast of work being done by German and French metallurgists by reading journals. Ellen's work with Robert was so significant that she was elected to the American Institute of Mining and Metallurgical Engineers as its first female member.

The Richards's home in Jamaica Plain was to be not only a home away from home for their students and other young people but also a living laboratory for Ellen's work in bringing scientific principles to everyday housekeeping and living. While warm and welcoming in atmosphere, their home embodied the sound principles of engineering and chemistry. Gone were the heavy drapes, carpets, and upholstery so popular in the Victorian era. In their place were hardwood floors softened by small rugs, windows framed in light curtains that let in fresh air, and a ventilating system that Robert designed. The cooking stove was powered by gas, not coal, and the floors were swept by a vacuum cleaner. This bright, airy, and efficient home also proved Ellen's theory that the home was society's most civilizing influence. A healthy and efficient home, she surmised, could be both a source of pride to a woman and a comfort to her family, without condemning the woman to perpetual servitude.

Adding a new dimension to homemaking and removing its drudgery became a mission for Ellen. She believed that women had actually been the losers as old-fashioned domestic skills had been replaced by manufacturing. They had lost the home arts—the spinning, weaving, and sewing—that gave them a productive and creative outlet—and kept only the boring, hard work of cleaning and cooking. But there was more to creating a productive and healthy home environment than scrubbing floors, and Ellen set out to help American women find it.

Her theory was that the more women knew about nutrition, food chemistry, health, pollutants, and other sciences of home-making, the more interesting—and effective—their work would become. Her intense interest in channeling scientific advances to home use, and to applying scientific and logical methods to running the home, led her to realize the greatest obstacle to this goal: Women were untrained in both scientific theory and practice. They were strangers to the laboratories where young men studied chemistry and physics and as a result, as Ellen once complained, didn't even understand why water wouldn't run uphill!

So, being the practical woman that she was, Ellen began her campaign for the scientific household by promoting science education for women. But before women could be taught sciences in every school, Ellen's ultimate goal, science teachers had to be trained. Since secondary schools lacked laboratories and teachers who could use them, science was taught only at higher levels not open to most women.

While she was still an undergraduate at MIT, Ellen was among those who taught a pilot chemistry course at Girls' High School in Boston. Many in the class were already teachers, and the course was sponsored in part by the Women's Education Association of Boston. When, in 1875, Ellen mounted her campaign in earnest, she appealed to the association for funding. Her goal was to establish a laboratory at MIT where women could study biology, chemistry, and mineralogy. In 1876 the laboratory opened in a building owned by MIT. Through Ellen's solicitations, the Women's Education Association outfitted the lab and provided textbooks and even scholarships that allowed women to attend classes. Ellen and Professor John Ordway, an industrial chemist with whom Ellen had worked while she was at MIT, taught courses there, both of them contributing their time and supporting the program with monetary contributions as well. Ellen donated about $1,000 a year, a considerable amount of money in the late 1800s.

One problem Ellen encountered was that many of the women who studied at the new laboratory had very limited preparation in the sciences and almost no laboratory experience. For many it was the first time they had been on their own, away from families and hometowns. Ellen became their mentor, advisor, and friend—an unofficial Dean of Women, of sorts. Along with advising them on their finances and helping with their studies, she cautioned them to be careful of the example they set. Ellen was always very conscious of the role these early women played in preparing the way for those women who would follow.

Ellen was never one to be content with one project at a time. While she was teaching and supporting the women's laboratory at MIT, she was also setting up a science component for the Society to Encourage Studies at Home, a correspondence school established to educate women. Ellen developed lasting friendships with some of the women she taught through this program, and in turn learned first-hand about the problems they faced. Health seemed to be a serious concern for the women she taught, many of whom were frequently ill. She wrote a booklet advocating physical exercise and proper diet, along with pursuits of the mind to counteract the stresses of running a household.

She joined with other educated women in the Boston area in 1882 to found the Association of Collegiate Alumnae, which would later become the American Association of University Women, an organization that promotes education for women to this day. Through this group and on her own, Ellen worked for better opportunities for women in graduate studies.

While Ellen was an undergraduate, she had worked as assistant to Professor William Nichols, who was analyzing the public water supply for the Massachusetts Board of Health. Here she had developed an interest in pollutants in water and other environmental hazards. Like Nichols, Professor Ordway—Ellen's colleague at the new MIT laboratory for women—consulted with government and private industry, and put Ellen in touch with several clients. Along with water supplies, she tested fabrics and wallpapers for arsenic, and other commercial products for dangerous contaminants or combustibility. One of the most interesting studies she undertook was one for the Massachusetts Board of Health to determine the purity of basic groceries sold in food shops.

She assigned her students enrolled in chemical analysis courses the task of testing basic food and household staples, including vinegar, soap powders, and other common ingredients and cleaning compounds. Some of their findings astonished even Ellen, who already had few illusions about the purity of foods. Her students found cinnamon composed of more than half mahogany dust, and baking powder that was almost half laundry starch. Their findings were discussed in her books *The Chemistry of Cooking and Cleaning: A Manual for House-keepers*, published in 1882, and *Food Materials and Their Adulterations*, published in 1885.

So smoothly did the women students blend into the academic life of MIT, that they were quickly accepted into regular classes alongside male students. Four had been awarded degrees by 1883, when the women's laboratory was closed and women were admitted to the college on an equal basis with men. At the urging and fundraising efforts of Ellen and several others, MIT included a women's study and parlor in one of their new buildings.

While Ellen's work on behalf of women at MIT was largely finished with the establishment of equal admission, she had plenty more missions to occupy her efforts. In 1884 the school set up a laboratory to study sanitation. It was the first of its kind anywhere, and its director was Ellen's old friend and colleague William Nichols. As before, Ellen was his assistant. This gave her a faculty position, that of Instructor in Sanitary Chemistry, a position she held for more than a quarter of a century. During a two-year analysis of water supplies in Massachusetts, Ellen directed the laboratory. The study was the first of its kind and became the standard for future water pollution investigations. Ellen supervised the testing of water samples, designing the equipment and developing the tests and record-keeping methods.

When MIT began the nation's first Sanitary Engineering program in 1890, Ellen taught air, water, and sewage analysis and co-authored the basic text in the subject, *Air, Water and Food for Colleges*, published in 1900. Her students went on to become leaders in the drive for public sanitation not only in the United States but all over the world.

For all her lofty work in bettering public sanitation and health, Ellen's heart was still in her spare-time work of improving the role of the housewife and making the scientifically managed home the goal of every woman. To this end, she envisioned a society that would value the work of women in running a home.

With this and her work in public health and sanitation came the increasing awareness of the plight of working-class families in the cities. Economic times were hard, and with the Depression came indifference among immigrants in inner-city neighborhoods: Children were no longer raised in an atmosphere of self-sufficiency, as farm and rural children had been previously. And with this loss of the manual skills that enabled families to provide for themselves came a sense of inadequacy and despair. A new generation was growing up amid a sense of helplessness. Instead of creating, they were consuming, and this worried those, like Ellen, with a social conscience. Food and nutrition, Ellen thought, were at the root of this. And at the very least, by improving the quality of food, the unemployed and underemployed city dwellers would be in better health and thus less liable to spread disease.

With the financial support of Pauline Agassiz Shaw, a Boston philanthropist, Ellen conducted a study on the food and nutrition of working men. The findings of the study led to the opening of the New England Kitchen in 1890. This public kitchen offered low-cost foods scientifically prepared, ready to take home and serve to a family. The emphasis was on a high nutrition-to-cost ratio and on the demonstration kitchen itself, where anyone could watch the food being prepared (and hopefully, adopt some of the scientific and efficient methods used there). The New England Kitchen drew a great deal of interest from philanthropists in other cities and was the model for later ones in Chicago, New York, Providence, and elsewhere. The foods served—fish chowder, baked beans, rice pudding, beef stew—appealed to affluent Bostonians, who appreciated the well-prepared favorites and were happy to take advantage of the low prices. But the kitchen was not a success. No one anticipated the resistance of immigrant communities, which made up most of the poor that the kitchen was intended to serve, to the bland, one-flavor-fits-all dishes served. While highly nutritious, the meals lacked appeal to ethnic tastes used to more highly flavored foods.

From the New England Kitchen, however, grew the idea of an exhibit for the 1893 Chicago World's Fair. Ellen created there the Rumford Kitchen, with demonstrations of modern cooking, exhibits on balanced diet, and a lunchroom where nutritious meals were served. The exhibit drew a lot of attention and was among the most popular of the fair.

The following year the Boston school system contracted with the New England Kitchen to provide school lunches. School systems, hospitals, and various institutions consulted with the organization to improve meal preparation methods and the nutritive quality of menus. From all this grew a demand for experts in diet, the beginnings of dietetics as a career field. Ellen took all of these demonstrable proofs to mean that dietitians would be required in the future, and she continued her campaign for the addition of domestic science courses in public schools. As a member of the Women's Education Association's Committee on Public Schools, she worked for public support of a science and arts high school for girls, and for adding domestic science as a core course for girls in public schools. She was more successful in creating a school of homemaking at the Women's Educational and Industrial Union in 1899. This later became the Home Economics Department at Simmons College.

The term "home economics" was not in use at the turn of the twentieth century. In 1899 Ellen and others assembled at a summer conference in Lake Placid, New York, to discuss the field of domestic sciences. One of their first acts was to decide on a more professional name for all the sciences and arts used in operating a household. They chose "home economics" as the most accurate description, and it became the proper academic term. The meetings were held for several summers as the Lake Placid Conference on Home Economics, and under Ellen's leadership as chairperson, they outlined course curricula for high schools, colleges, and extension courses; set teachers' standards; and acted as a clearinghouse for information and ideas in the field. It was Ellen who was credited as the guiding light of these summer gatherings, which subsequently resulted in the American Home Economics Association. She was chosen as the first president of the association and remained its president until 1910. Ellen founded the association's *Journal of Home Economics* and paid for its publication herself.

The new discipline that was created and defined by the Lake Placid conferences and the American Home Economics Association positioned home economics as a recognized course of academic study based on science, economics, and sociology. In addition to the science of running a household, the group encompassed the economics of production and consumption in the marketplace. Ellen pointed out that the role of the twentieth-century homemaker had changed, and that educating consumers was as much a part of her work as keeping microbes from under the kitchen sink.

Ellen coined two new words that are still in use today. The first is "euthenics"—the study of improving the whole environment in its social, moral, and physical aspects. The second, although spelled differently today, is "oekology," the science of studying the relationship and balance between various parts of an environment. Ellen used this term to describe the many forces at play in creating a healthy, nurturing home environment. We know the concept today—in a broader sense—as the science of ecology.

Ellen's work in the field of home economics made her a popular speaker, and she always welcomed the chance to spread her message on the need for better education in homemaking and the training of science teachers. This work, and the eighteen books she wrote, gained her an honorary doctor of science degree from Smith College and a seat on the council of the National Education Association, with responsibility for their policies on teaching home economics.

Her life was filled with work until she died at her Boston home following a heart attack in 1911. She was sixty-eight years old, and had just completed writing her address on applied sciences for MIT's fiftieth anniversary celebration.

Ellen's legacy lives on in classrooms and school science laboratories across the nation, where home economics is part of the standard curriculum, and female students work side by side with males as equals in chemistry, physics, and biology.

• • •

Ellen Richards's papers are at Smith College Library, Northampton, in the Sophia Smith Collection.

Her grave at Christ Church Yard in Gardiner, Maine, is marked by a stone inscribed with words her husband chose: "Pioneer—Educator—Scientist—An Earnest Seeker—A Tireless Worker—A Thoughtful Friend—A Helper of Mankind."

Fannie Merritt Farmer

1857–1915

Teaching Women to Cook

*W*ell, Miss Farmer, much as we admire your proposal, I cannot imagine that women would buy another cookbook. Why, there must be at least ten on the market already!"

"But mine will treat cooking in a scientific way, with recipes using careful step-by-step directions, precise measurements, exact cooking times and temperatures. The results of each recipe will be predictable even for the inexperienced cook."

"Do you really think all this detail is necessary, Miss Farmer?" the editor replied. "After all, is cooking not something every little girl learns at her mother's side? Perhaps a few women would buy this book, but surely not enough for us to make a profit by publishing it."

Fannie Merritt Farmer had one last fallback plan ready. "Very well," she persisted. "If I were to pay the expenses of publishing the book, would you consider it?"

The editor leaned back in his leather chair and looked out the large window of the brownstone building on Beacon Street, his gaze sweeping across Boston Common. This was no ordinary woman, he knew. She was the director of the Boston Cooking

Fannie Farmer (second row, third from the left) and women from the Class of 1900 at the Boston Cooking School

School, a well-respected institution begun by culinary expert Mary Lincoln. If she were to pay all the publisher's costs herself, how could he go wrong? If the book sold, he would make a profit. If it didn't, there was nothing to lose.

"Under those circumstances, Miss Farmer, we will accept your book for publication."

Fannie rose, thanked the editor, and limped from his office. He smiled at his success in signing on a book without any financial risk to Little, Brown & Co.

If he could have looked into the future, his smile might have been even broader, for *The Boston Cooking-School Cook Book* was to make millions of dollars for the publisher over the next century, continuing into twelve editions of what would become America's kitchen Bible.

Fannie's mission to teach American women to cook appetizing and nutritious meals had begun late in life, at least for a woman of the late 1800s. She had begun her career at thirty-one, twelve years after a disabling illness had interrupted her high school education.

Fannie was born in Boston, the eldest of four surviving daughters of John and Mary Farmer. Her father, who was known as J. Franklin Farmer, was a successful printer, but his reluctance to upgrade to modern printing technology cost his business dearly. Despite their diminishing resources, the Farmers felt strongly about educating their girls.

Fannie and her sisters attended school in Medford, where her family moved when she was a child. She was a very good student, and her parents intended to send her on to college. They were greatly disappointed when a paralysis of her legs at age sixteen forced her to leave Medford High School. Although it is now difficult to be certain, her affliction is generally thought to have been polio. It has also been suggested that the injury might have been the result of a stroke, since years later Fannie suffered a stroke that increased this paralysis. The young Fannie was confined to bed for many months and was unable to walk for several years. When she could once again walk, it was with a noticeable limp. Although she had been an excellent student and had a bright and enquiring mind, her disability and lack of a diploma made it almost impossible for her to find work. Marriage was similarly unlikely, since any disability in those days was thought to make a woman an unsuitable wife.

In her twenties and unwilling to remain a drain on her family's already tight finances, Fannie found work as a mother's helper to the Shaw family. She was always determined that her limp would not limit her, and she never used it as an excuse to get out of doing her share. The Shaw's lived in nearby Cambridge, and Fannie took care of their daughter Marcia. Many accounts of Fannie's first interest in standard measurements include a story about how Marcia watched Fannie cook and asked her what "butter the size of an egg" meant. Another, more likely, story suggests that it was a similar question from a later student that set her on the quest for precise measurement.

It was her interest in cooking which she developed during her work for the Shaw family, which prompted both the Shaws and her parents to suggest that she enroll in the Boston Cooking School and become a cooking teacher. A high school diploma was not required for admission, nor was one necessary to teach cooking.

Fannie was by this time thirty-one, and excited to at last have a career in front of her. This eagerness to work and her facility for learning drew the attention of her teachers almost at once. They were so impressed with Fannie's skill and enthusiasm for cooking that when she completed the course, the school asked her to become the assistant to its principal, Carrie Dearborn. After Fannie spent two years in this post, where she had been given increased responsibilities, Dearborn resigned in 1893 to become a food lecturer. The board of the Boston Cooking School immediately offered the position of principal to Fannie, who accepted happily.

The job was not without its immediate challenges. The school had been founded by the well-known cook and lecturer Mary Lincoln. Lincoln was the author of the best-known cookbook of the day, *Mrs. Lincoln's Boston Cook Book*, which gave the school even greater fame and cachet. But when Lincoln resigned in 1885 to pursue her writing and lecturing full time, there was no one of her reputation and ability to keep the school in the public eye, and the school began to fall into debt.

Carrie Dearborn had begun to bring the school back to its past glory, but it was still on shaky financial footing when Fannie became its principal. She set about immediately to restore its place in the public eye as the center of everything new and modern in cooking. If the school was to be what it had once been, she felt, it had to prove that women needed to learn modern cooking methods and nutrition in order to feed their families well and keep them healthy.

The first message Fannie brought to the students was her own personal philosophy that anyone who tried could learn to cook well. It was not a talent you were born with but one anyone could acquire. And the Boston Cooking School was the place to do it. This enthusiastic teacher told her students: If a cook can make a few basic dishes well, she can cook almost anything. Along with knowing how to serve a balanced diet to her family, Fannie thought that a good cook should know how to make it appetizing and appealing to eat. She urged the students to do more than boil their vegetables but to treat them as specialty dishes, adding their own touch. She developed attractive ways to serve common dishes, along with ways to vary them.

"Dressing up" foods with garnishes, serving them in what we would now consider fussy arrangements, and using sauces to vary their flavors not only made food more appealing to eat but made its preparation less monotonous. All this attention to the art and science of cooking was part of Fannie's greater goal of lifting women out of the position of household drudge by showing them how to cook not just well but enthusiastically. No one exceeded Fannie in creating (and delighting in) fanciful food fripperies. Fannie played with her food, to the delight of her students and readers, creating birds and animals with peppercorn eyes and dabbing whipped foam on the top of a gelatin dessert glass to simulate the head on beer.

Although busy with the day-to-day operations of running a school, Fannie brought attention to the Boston Cooking School in articles, cooking demonstrations, and lectures, where she preached this message: "It is impossible," she reminded readers in a *Women's*

Home Companion article, "to raise cookery above a mere drudgery if one does not put heart and soul into the work; then, and only then, it becomes the most enjoyable of household duties."

It is important to remember that in the late 1800s, the word "gourmet" was little understood outside of France. Plain, boiled dinners—well suited to wood stoves and large families—were the norm. Food was more a necessity than a joy. But modern conveniences such as reliable stoves, refrigeration, and availability of out-of-season ingredients were beginning to change the American kitchen. Fannie was instrumental in this evolution and urged her students to take advantage of all that science and technology could offer them, and to do it with verve and gusto.

All the while Fannie was pondering the problem of uniform measurements. Recipes at this time called for amounts such as "a pinch" or "a handful" or in terms of some supposedly standard size. Butter measurement was described as the size of an egg or a walnut, even though eggs could vary greatly in size. Teaspoons, soup spoons, and teacups were favorite measuring implements in American kitchens, although even these varied in size. And it was never clear how much of a dry ingredient was to be used when the recipe called for "heaping." Others had complained about this system of quasi-measurement, too, including domestic expert Lillian Betts, who wrote in 1895 that "The Housekeeper must fit herself to separate the chaff from the wheat when reading them [cookbooks], and if she is wise she will cull the best into a book of her own, after experiment and investigation."

It was exactly this kind of experimentation that Fannie thought the busy cook should not have to do. Taking the guesswork out of measuring ingredients became her mission. It was this inexactitude that kept the average or beginning cook from turning out predictable dishes every time, and Fannie was determined to find a better way. Measuring ingredients with precision was not the only exactitude she strove for. Cooking times and temperatures were just as important. "A quick oven" was just as vague as "a heaping teacup" to an inexperienced cook, and Fannie was among the first to applaud modern ovens with thermometers.

Although Fannie did not invent the standardized measuring cup (measures for half pints—one cup—had become available only a few years earlier and measuring spoons not long thereafter), she was the first cookbook author to insist on their use and to use level measurements. Her predecessors, if they had used these "new-fangled" measures at all, had still used them inexactly, as "rounded" and "heaping" spoonfuls. Fannie leveled off their tops with a knife blade, leaving no room for inexact measurements.

Fannie was thirty-nine when she took her manuscript, complete with standardized and carefully tested measurements, to Little, Brown's Beacon Street offices and gambled her savings to print 3,000 copies. In its preface she expressed her own hope for a better understanding of nutrition: "I certainly feel that a time is not far distant when a knowledge of the principles of diet will be an essential part of one's education."

Her confidence in her work, and in the eagerness of the American housewife to turn out reliably good meals day after day, was justified, and *The Boston Cooking-School Cook Book*, published in 1896, was an immediate success. The following year it sold out two more printings and continued to sell a printing each year until its first revision in 1906. This, too, was reprinted annually, with each printing numbering 20,000. By the time of her death in 1915, Fannie's cookbook had sold more than a third of a million copies.

That is not to imply that the cookbook was universally praised. Fannie's book was published after *Mrs. Lincoln's Boston Cook Book*, by Mary Lincoln, founder of the Boston Cooking School, which had been used up until then as the school's textbook. Lincoln, then editor of *New England Kitchen Magazine*, noted that Fannie's book relied heavily on recipes in the school's—and her own book's—repertoire. Lincoln mentioned in her review of the book in an 1897 issue of her magazine that the teachers and cookbooks that preceded this new arrival should be remembered. She even suggested that she and the previous principals of the school should have been credited. In her review she failed to mention the overriding difference between the publications—that the new book's recipes had been carefully tested and ascribed standard measurements.

Fannie not only liked to cook, she liked to eat. As often as possible she dined in Boston's best restaurants and those of cities where she was lecturing. She was adept at identifying ingredients and flavors, which she would record and absorb into her own repertoire. When she was unable to identify the ingredients of a sauce, she was not above dabbing a few drops onto a calling card and taking it back to the school for analysis. She encouraged her students to sample dishes of established chefs and experiment with replicating them. "Could it be better?" This was the question with which Fannie continually challenged her students and fellow teachers. Even when building on the creations of well-known culinarians, she was always striving for the best result. Her niece-in-law, Wilma Lord Perkins, who revised her cookbook through its eleventh edition, remembers that this favorite phrase of Fannie's "sometimes caused at least temporary dismay to her devoted teachers and helpers but to which they always responded with skill and pride."

In 1904 *The Women's Home Companion* asked each of six well-known women in the cooking field—cookbook authors, cooking magazine writers and editors, and cooking teachers—to write an article called "My Twelve Favorite Recipes." Among the group were Fannie and her illustrious predecessor and founder of the Boston Cooking School, Mary Lincoln. This was formidable company. Fannie decided that this was a good platform for her to proclaim her mantra of appealing presentation and tasty sauces. Her timbales and fish filets were richly sauced, and paper frills decorated another dish. "Brazilian Salad"—created especially for the article—was a takeoff on Waldorf Salad, substituting brazil nuts for walnuts and grapes and pineapple for apples. This she served in a "box" made of saltine crackers. Caramel bisque ice cream and a birthday cake made an ambitious finale. Her recipes were so clear and precise that they were by far the most popular ones in the article.

As a result of the article, published in February 1905, *The Women's Home Companion* asked Fannie to write a regular cooking column. Although the least known of the six panelists, Fannie had already outstripped them as the up and coming voice in American cooking. And in doing so, she provided herself with a regular forum to promote her ideas and her cooking school.

By this time Fannie had become restless at the Boston Cooking School, whose board saw the school's function as training cooking teachers, not cooks themselves. In 1902, after eleven years there, Fannie left the school. Sadly, the Boston Cooking School, without Fannie's name and reputation to carry it, floundered and closed the following year.

Fannie moved on and soon opened Miss Farmer's School of Cookery. To assist her, she hired five teachers early on, but soon added five more. Fannie specialized in teaching cooking to women about to be married, and private cooks who were sent by the wealthy Boston families that employed them. Classes were divided into skill levels and subjects, progressing from the basics to elegant dinners for entertaining. Special classes were added to teach women how to choose and buy food, and how to cook for the sick.

Along with private lessons and regular classes, Fannie held cooking lectures. On Wednesday mornings the audience was filled with home cooks, and in the evening, professional cooks. Immensely popular, the lectures attracted audiences of up to 250 and were reported on in the following day's *Evening Transcript*, which syndicated the detailed articles—complete with recipes—all over the country.

Soon Fannie's sister Cora joined her in preparing the monthly column for *The Women's Home Companion*, which included a menu with recipes each month. Meanwhile Fannie worked on additional books: *What to Have for Dinner* (1905), *Catering for Social Occasions with Menus and Recipes* (1911), and *A New Book of Cookery* (1912), along with revisions of her original 1896 cookbook. In addition she traveled all over the country to lecture to women's clubs and other audiences.

Having established standardized measurements and cooking temperatures as part of recipes, Fannie turned to another interest, making it her mission to improve the food that was served to the disabled. This was a subject she knew from both perspectives, since she herself had been bedridden for several years and knew how deeply a patient's mood could affect eating and hence recovery. Along with studying the latest findings in nutrition and digestion, Fannie advocated teasing the patient's appetite with creative presentations, individual molded servings, pretty garnishes, and elegant touches that would encourage the ill to look forward to the next meal. After writing her book *Food and Cookery for the Sick and Convalescent* (the book that she considered to be her most important work), she offered lectures to hospital dieticians, gave short courses to nurses, and addressed students at Harvard Medical School. Dr. Elliot P. Joslin, a pioneer in diabetes research, credited Fannie with inspiring his own writings.

By 1913, at age fifty-six, Fannie's own health began to fail. Never one to slow down because of her health, she kept right on going at her usual pace until she suffered two strokes and was once again unable to walk. Even then, she continued to lecture from a wheelchair until a week before her death, January 15, 1915. Fannie was fifty-eight years old.

Although Fannie died a wealthy woman by that day's standards, she left a legacy far greater than her estate. To generations of homemakers and cooks Fannie left standardized measurements, times, and cooking temperatures, and a cookbook that has endured for more than a century. Since her death nearly a century ago, five generations of cooks have answered their questions and found their recipes by reaching for "Fannie Farmer."

• • •

Fannie Merritt Farmer is buried, along with many other distinguished Bostonians, in Mount Auburn Cemetery in Cambridge.

Her *Boston Cooking-School Cook Book,* now in its twelfth edition, has been for the last several editions entitled *The Fannie Farmer Cookbook,* bringing its official title in line with the name by which it has been informally known since her own time.

BIBLIOGRAPHY

GENERAL SOURCES

Adamson, Lynda G. *Notable Women in American History: A Guide to Recommended Biographies and Autobiographies.* Westport, Conn.: Greenwood Press, 1999.

Otten, Laura A. *Women's Rights and the Law.* Westport, Conn.: Praeger Publishers, 1993.

Wright, Richardson. *Forgotten Ladies: Nine Portraits from the American Family Album.* Philadelphia: J. B. Lippincot & Co., 1928.

ELIZABETH "MUMBET" FREEMAN

Chase, Arthur C. *The Ashleys: A Pioneer Berkshire Family.* Beverly, Mass.: The Trustees of Reservations, 1982.

"Elizabeth 'Mumbet' Freeman." Online. www.mumbet.com.

Felton, Harold W. *Mumbet: The Story of Elizabeth Freeman.* New York: Dodd Mead, 1970.

Sedgwick, John. "The Eternity Club." *New England Monthly,* September 1989.

Tinling, Marion. *Women Remembered: A Guide to Landmarks of Women's History in the United States.* Westport, Conn.: Greenwood Press, 1986.

Wilds, Mary. *Mumbet: The Life and Times of Elizabeth Freeman: The True Story of a Slave Who Won Her Freedom.* Greensboro, N.C., Avisson Publishers, Inc., 1999.

ABIGAIL ADAMS

Butterfield, L. H., Marc Friedlaender, and Mary-Jo Kline. *The Book of Abigail and John: Selected Letters of the Adams Family, 1762–1784.* Cambridge, Mass.: Harvard University Press, 1975.

BIBLIOGRAPHY

Caroli, Betty Boyd. *First Ladies*. New York: Oxford University Press, 1995.

Levin, Phyllis Lee. *Abigail Adams: A Biography*. New York: Thomas Dunne Books, 2001.

Withey, Lynne. *Dearest Friend*. New York: Simon and Schuster, 2001.

DEBORAH SAMSON

Campbell, Karlyn Kohrs. *Women Public Speakers in the United States, 1800–1925: A Bio-Critical Sourcebook*. Westport, Conn.: Greenwood Press, 1993.

"Deborah Samson." Online. www.canton.org/samson/. Canton Massachusetts Historical Society.

Freeman, Lucy, and Alma Halbert Bond. *America's First Woman Warrior: The Courage of Deborah Sampson*. New York: Paragon House, 1992.

Mann, Herman. *The Female Review, or Memoirs of an American Young Lady*. New York: Arno Press, 1972.

"Notable Women Ancestors." Online. www.rootsweb.com/~nwa/sampson .html.

ELIZABETH PALMER PEABODY

Ronda, Bruce. *Elizabeth Palmer Peabody: A Reformer on Her Own Terms*. Cambridge, Mass.: Harvard University Press, 1999.

Steele, Zulma. *Lives to Remember*. New York: Arno Press, 1974.

Tharp, Louise Hall. *The Peabody Sisters of Salem*. Boston: Little, Brown and Company, 1950.

THE MILL GIRLS: LUCY LARCOM AND SARAH BAGLEY

Bushman, Claudia. *A Good Poor Man's Wife*. Hanover, N.H.: University Press of New England, 1981.

BIBLIOGRAPHY

Moran, William. *The Belles of New England: The Women of the Textile Mills and the Families Whose Wealth They Wove.* New York: St. Martin's Press, 2002.

Selden, Bernice. *The Mill Girls.* New York: Athenaeum, 1983

ELEANOR CREESY

Carse, Robert. *Moonrakers.* New York: Harper & Brothers, 1961.

Lyon, Margaret, and Flora Elizabeth Reynolds. *The* Flying Cloud *and Her First Passengers.* Oakland, Calif.: The Center for the Book, Mills College, 1992.

Shaw, David. Flying Cloud: *The True Story of America's Most Famous Clipper Ship and the Woman Who Guided Her.* New York: William Morrow, 2000.

MARIA MITCHELL

Maria Mitchell Association. Online. www.mmo.org.

Wright, Helen. *Sweeper in the Sky: The Life of Maria Mitchell, First Woman Astronomer in America.* New York: Macmillan Co., 1949.

JULIA WARD HOWE

Howe, Julia Ward. *Reminiscences.* Cambridge, Mass.: Riverside Press, 1899.

Richards, Laura E., and Maude Howe Elliot. *Julia Ward Howe 1819–1910.* Cambridge, Mass.: Riverside Press, 1916.

Williams, Gary. *Hungry Heart: The Literary Emergence of Julia Ward Howe.* Boston: University of Massachusetts Press, 1999.

ELLEN SWALLOW RICHARDS

Hunt, Caroline. *The Life of Ellen H. Richards.* Boston: Whitcomb and Barrows, 1912.

BIBLIOGRAPHY

Richards, Ellen. Papers. Sophia Smith Collection. Smith College Library, Northampton, Mass.

Richards, Ellen, and S. Maria Elliot. *The Chemistry of Cooking and Cleaning.* Boston: Whitcomb and Barrows, 1882.

Shapiro, Laura. *Perfection Salad: Women and Cooking at the Turn of the Century.* New York: Farrar, Straus and Giroux, 1986.

Wylie, Francis E. "The First Oekologist." In *The New England Galaxy: The Best of 20 Years from Old Sturbridge Village,* edited by Roger Parks. Chester, Conn.: The Globe Pequot Press, 1980.

FANNIE MERRITT FARMER

The Arthur and Elizabeth Schlesinger Library, Radcliffe College, Cambridge, Mass. www.radcliffe.edu/schles (for all editions of cookbooks by Fanny Farmer).

Farmer, Fannie. *The Fannie Farmer Cookbook.* Revised by Wilma Lord Perkins. Boston: Little Brown, editions since 1896.

Lynes, Russell. *American Heritage Cookbook.* Vol. I. New York: American Heritage Publishing, 1964.

Shapiro, Laura. *Perfection Salad: Women and Cooking at the Turn of the Century.* New York: Farrar, Straus and Giroux, 1986.

Simmons College Archive, Boston, www.simmonscollege.edu/libraries (records of the Boston Cooking School).

INDEX

INDEX

INDEX

Warren, Mercy Otis, 13, 14, 17,
    21, 25
Washington, George, 32, 33
West Street Bookshop, The, 48–49
What to Have for Dinner, 126
Woman's Peace Congress, 98
Women
    and education, 44–45, 49,
      59–60, 110
    in eighteenth century, 76
    equal rights, 14–15, 21–22, 61,
      82, 100

    and patriotism, 36
    place in society, 99–100
    right to vote, 101
Women's Educational and
    Industrial Union, 114
Women's Education Association,
    109, 114
Women's Home Companion, The,
    121–22, 124, 125, 126
Words for the Hour, 97
Workers' rights, 54–64

About The Author

Lura Rogers Seavey is a New England native with a special interest in writing children's nonfiction. She is the coauthor of *Fun with the Family in Vermont and New Hampshire* (Globe Pequot Press) and writes for several periodicals, including *New Hampshire Magazine*.